Insider Tips For Getting The Best Price

The Complete Guide To Selling Your Toronto Condo

Learn How To Sell Your Toronto Condo For Top Dollar Fast

Thomas Cook

ISBN-10: 1545317054
ISBN-13: 978-1545317051

ARE YOU ALSO A TORONTO CONDO OR HOUSE BUYER?

If you are, you might benefit greatly from reading one or both of these books too

Get a clear understanding about everything you need to know when buying a Toronto condo or house

Free download at…

UltimateHomeBuyersGuide.com

Avoid costly mistakes when getting pre-approved for a mortgage

Free download at…

HomeBuyersFinancingGuide.com

ABOUT THE AUTHOR

Let's start off by giving you a little background about where I'm coming from in terms of experience and knowledge. I've been in the real estate industry since 1980. While originally with Royal LePage, I switched to RE/MAX Hallmark in 1983, where I have been ever since.

Along with helping literally thousands of people to buy and sell their homes, over the years I've been involved in a number of other real estate related activities as well. For example, through the '80s I had a property management company and at times managed up to 350 single-family homes, duplexes, triplexes, condos, and small four- and eight-unit buildings, mainly for investors but often for people who were out of the city on a job transfer and wanted to maintain their existing residence.

That has provided some great insight into such things as tenant related issues, understanding of the Tenant Protection Act, and knowledge on how to design a really good rental application and a comprehensive lease. I find those things help today with clients who are interested in buying something that has a rental component to it — maybe the traditional basement rental apartment where the owner lives upstairs, or more likely today a downtown Toronto condominium suite.

I've renovated about twenty-five homes in Toronto, as well as building a triplex from the ground up in Riverdale. In 2008, I built a cottage in the Kawarthas that started with an uncleared lot. These experiences certainly provided some great insights into working with contractors, dealing with City Hall for building permits, and even on occasion going to the Committee of Adjustment or the OMB (Ontario Municipal Board) when obtaining a permit requires applying for a variance.

I find these experiences help with clients who might be interested in buying something that needs renovation or fix up work. For example, a common question that both house and condo buyers ask is, "Can we take out that wall between the kitchen and the dining room? We'd like to have a more open concept there. Is that a structural wall? And if it is, how do we open it up and support it so we don't damage the integrity of the entire structure while we're doing that?"

I can certainly offer advice and answer those kinds of questions for my clients — and many more.

For several years, I also had a mortgage company, which provided a lot of insight into mortgage financing. As a result, I'm quite knowledgeable about how to package the buyer's mortgage application to get clients the best possible rate and terms along the way.

Here's How To Get In Touch...

Thomas Cook
Real Estate Sales Representative @ RE/MAX Hallmark Realty Ltd Brokerage

Mobile | 647-962-1650
Office | 416-465-7850

LivingInToronto.com
Direct | Thomas@LivingInToronto.com

Author of the 'Ultimate Home Buyer's Guide', the 'Home Buyer's Financing Guide' and other informative real estate publications and reports

Experience | | Thousands of homes sold since 1980
Professional Designations | | ABR, SRES
Awards | | RE/MAX's 2ND highest award - Circle Of Legends
Charity Support | | Over $115,000 contributed to the Toronto Sick Kids Hospital
Speaker & Agent Coach | | Delivered seminars and presentations to the public and Realtors about buying and selling real estate since 1995

ARE YOU THINKING OF SELLING YOUR TORONTO CONDOMINIUM THIS YEAR OR NEXT?

By reading this book you're on your way to helping yourself have a successful sale and getting the highest price possible. As the saying goes 'Knowledge Is Power'.

I've compiled the book contents from my 37+ years of experience of successfully helping buyers and sellers in the Toronto real estate market. We've sold over 2500 homes in that time and some years we did almost $100,000,000 in total house and condo sales.

I've worked through three recessions since 1980 and now one of the longest stretches of market appreciation in Toronto's history.

So, I've seen it all... extreme buyer's markets and now extreme seller's markets... but in every instance, a competent, knowledgeable Realtor adds value to every seller when they're ready to enter the market.

In this book, I will be telling you how my Team and I approach selling Toronto homes. Of course, we'd love to work with every single one of you in your condo or house sale, but sometimes that's not possible. Your condo might be in Hamilton or Oshawa or another geographic area that we don't service. So, take advantage of the information I'm sharing with you here and use it as a benchmark or a guideline when you are looking for a listing agent to represent you.

Of course, when selling your Toronto condominium, you always have four choices...

- You could decide to do nothing... after hearing what the market is doing and finding out what your suite is worth right now, you may make the decision to hold onto your condo

- You could try to sell your condo yourself... every year about 5% of Toronto sales are made by owners selling on their own
- You may decide to work with one of the 54,000+ agents now registered with the Toronto Real Estate Board, many of which have very little if any experience in all the facets of properly and effectively marketing a home
- OR you may decide to work with a 'By Referral Only' Realtor like myself... someone whose goal is to provide such exceptional service that you'll feel compelled to refer all your friends and family for years to come

So, read on, build your knowledge and, if you feel like I've added some value to you, please feel free to contact me anytime with your questions.

Thomas Cook
Real Estate Sales Representative

Author | Ultimate Toronto Home Buyer's Guide
Author | Toronto Home Buyer's Financing Guide
Author | Free Government Money Report

LivingInToronto.com

CONTENTS

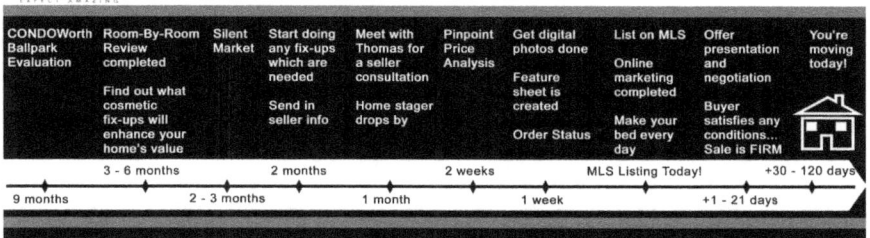

CONDOWorth Ballpark Evaluation	Room-By-Room Review completed	Silent Market	Start doing any fix-ups which are needed	Meet with Thomas for a seller consultation	Pinpoint Price Analysis	Get digital photos done	List on MLS	Offer presentation and negotiation	You're moving today!
	Find out what cosmetic fix-ups will enhance your home's value		Send in seller info	Home stager drops by		Feature sheet is created	Online marketing completed	Buyer satisfies any conditions...	
						Order Status	Make your bed every day	Sale is FIRM	

3 - 6 months		2 months		2 weeks		MLS Listing Today!		+30 - 120 days
9 months	2 - 3 months		1 month		1 week		+1 - 21 days	

CHAPTER 1
HOME SELLER TIMELINE EXPLAINED

People approach selling their properties with multiple timelines… some make a snap decision and want it on the market the day after tomorrow while others know the time is coming and they give themselves a few weeks and sometimes even a month or two to get the home prepared for sale.

There is certainly no minimum built into the system. A home owner could sign the paperwork tonight and be on the MLS tomorrow morning - maybe not the best idea because the marketing might not be complete, or even started, but it could be done.

The selling process works best if you allow some lead time before the listing is loaded onto the Toronto Real Estate Board (TREB) MLS system.

Let's look at the timeline above which is a demonstration of how we like to progress with our seller clients at whatever pace works for them.

Many sellers start off with just a random thought of moving so they go online several month ahead of their listing date to start researching home values.

The next question that typically crosses their mind is 'What improvements or fix-ups should I do to maximize my sale price?'. Here's where some expert advice comes in handy because we've seen owners spend more money than they should have doing upgrades which the buying public may not like or which may not be necessary.

We've created what we call a Room-By-Room Review where we do a walk-through of your home with you. We'll suggest cosmetic-only fix-ups and answer your questions as to what other changes or improvements would bring you a better return on the money you spend.

Some sellers have been open to having a limited number of qualified buyers access their home before it officially goes on the market... we call it our 'Silent Market'. Since we have a large database of buyers, this less stressful and less intrusive way of getting a home sold appeals to some sellers.

Once the Room-By-Room Review has been done, the seller now knows very specifically what they need to do to get prepared for selling and they can typically attach a realistic timeline to it. It may be just a few days or it might be a few weeks or even months before the things on the fix-up / cleanup list can be completed. No problem... whatever works best.

When the time comes to put the home officially on the market, the next step is to have a Seller Consultation where we'll review the fix-ups that have been completed, talk about current market conditions, go over our marketing plan and look at comparable sales that have happened recently.

Then the listing documents are signed and we've got a specific date set for when the home is going to be listed for sale officially. Our marketing program is put in place and is ready for that listing date.

We'll look at offers as per our seller's instructions and of course, negotiate on their behalf.

The closing date is usually within 30-60 days of the offer acceptance date although shorter or longer closings are possible.

CHAPTER 2
BEWARE OF AWKWARD SENSORY EXPERIENCES DESTROYING YOUR SALE

How do you think your condominium suite, or building for that matter, will stand up to an examination by every buyer's senses... sight, smell, hearing, feel and taste? Well, maybe not taste so much but certainly by the other four.

Prospective purchasers will have those four senses turned on high when they enter your building, take the elevator to your floor and then enter into your suite. Because your home is new to them, they're excited to experience what it would be like to live there full time.

When you are finalizing your preparations to put your home on the market, take two tours of your residence... one in the daytime and the other at night... and turn your personal 'sense meters' on high and pay attention to what you notice.

Sight is the big one of course... is the building lobby clean and immaculate? How does your unit show? Is it drab and boring to look at or are there some occasional bright colours to spice it up?

Check along baseboards and up on ceiling light fixtures and fans... are there cobwebs dangling or dust bunnies gathering in corners?

Before analyzing each room, make sure light bulbs are the appropriate wattage and work properly. I don't recommend using compact fluorescent bulbs (CFL's) when selling since the light they throw isn't that attractive.

Then, look closely at the walls for scratches, marks, missing or broken light switch plates, and mold or mildew. Are hanging pictures dusted and the glass cleaned?

They will take note of what the temperature feels like. Is it cold in the winter or hot in the summer? Contrary to what we say generally, if your condo faces south or west and gets a lot of summer sun, you might need to close the blinds somewhat at least and turn the AC up to limit how hot it gets.

Assess if there are any odours lingering in the hallways adjacent to your suite. You might have to try applying a little Fabreze to see if that will correct the situation. Remember not to cook smelly foods inside your condo while it's on the market. Some odours are not attractive to other ethnicities.

Often banishing odors takes little more than identifying the cause – cigarette smoke and butts, old tennis shoes, pets, dirty litter boxes – then cleaning and freshening the area. Smelling smoke inside a home is a big no-no for most buyers and we don't want your home to put off any purchaser while it is on the market.

Similarly, some buyers are not comfortable with any kinds of pets but most commonly it's dogs or cats that may cause discomfort. The best suggestion is to send pets to live elsewhere while showings are happening. Remove the litterbox and any pet toys that may be lying around.

Clean your window blinds and carpets, open windows and doors to allow fresh air to come in and replace odours with lightly scented candles or potpourri.

Are there minor or major noises occurring throughout your home? After you've lived in a home for just a few weeks, it's fairly typical for most of us to just tune out background noises. Streetcars rumbling by, highway traffic and ambulance sirens are the big ones but we also need to tune in to the smaller ones… a rattle in the back of the fridge, a drip, drip from the kitchen tap, a running toilet in the bathroom, a squeaky door hinge etc.

You can't do anything about those exterior noises other than by shutting any sliding glass doors and windows. At least you can demonstrate that if people do want quiet, they can have it with everything closed up. But you will have to try and deal with any interior noises you can detect.

Now that you've done your own 'sensory tour' and solved any problems you've found, ask a friend to do the same tour to make sure you haven't missed anything.

Paying attention to the small details before showings start will help make your condo stand out from the competition.

CHAPTER 3
BEING BEAUTIFUL MATTERS
NO MATTER THE SIZE

Typical condominium bathrooms are not large, unless you're in a 1,500 sf+ suite, but, no matter the size, you still want your bathroom(s) to show well.

When we, or a tenant, are in residence, it's normal for countertops to become cluttered with personal hygiene items, the bathroom sink to show the stains from an electric toothbrush spray and the shower area to display old soap residue and maybe even bits of black mould on the grout between tiles. But for sure that's not how we want it to look when you open up your home to buyers.

The presentation goal is to do a bathroom makeover comprised of a thorough cleaning of walls, ceilings, floors and fixtures, a fix-up of any missing grout, peeling paint and leaky plumbing connections and last a minimalist staging for walls and counters.

The first step is to remove everything that's there now on counters and inside any drawers, medicine cabinets or linen closets. Eliminate anything that you haven't used in the last 3-6 months including old medications.

Now that everything is out, it's time for elbow grease and a heavy-duty, thorough cleaning of the complete bathroom.

Sometimes you'll discover that, once the clutter under your sink has been removed, there's been a small leak from your drain going on for some time. Check and repair all fittings and, if your tap set is showing signs of wear, replace it with a modern version. You'll probably wish you'd done this earlier so you could have enjoyed it more yourself!

If the toilet tank has been running continuously, it's time to switch out the offending interior parts so it's operating correctly. If the tank cover or toilet seat have cracks, get a replacement.

Now to the tub and shower. A big no-no is black mould showing on the tiles or grout. One of the best cleaning methods is to fill a spray bottle with a 50-50 mix of vinegar and warm water. Spray it on and leave it for about 5 minutes and then scrub with a stiff brush. Even more powerful is to cover the grout with a paste of baking soda and water and then spray on the vinegar-water mix.

Scrub down the shower walls and replace any missing grout or peeling caulking.

If your shower shutoff handle is dripping, you may have to replace the cylinder inside. If the shower head is doing the same, perhaps it just needs a new washer OR go all out and buy an inexpensive snazzy rain-shower head from Home Depot.

Shower and bathroom ceilings often get peeling paint because the ceiling fan either isn't strong enough or wasn't turned on at shower time. This needs to be scraped, sanded, primed and painted using a mildew-resistant product.

Does your shower or sink drain slowly? It's typically because hair or other gunk has collected in the drain trap. If you're handy, take a metal coat hanger and straighten it out and then make a small hook at the end. Shove the hook end down into the pipe and catch any hair that's there. Keep at it several times to get as much as you can and then rinse with lots of water.

To get the final cleaning done, use a drain cleaner but be sure to follow the instructions closely!

A final touch, if you have a shower curtain rod, is to switch your old one out for a curved model that gives more room inside the shower. Spring for a brand new, light coloured shower curtain to hang on it.

Now it's time to stage your bathroom for the buyers. Keep it minimalist and put only three items on the counter top - something with a good smell, a new soap dispenser and maybe a small plant.

Are your floor mats and towels up to snuff? If not, ditch the old ones and head out to buy replacements. You'll be able to use them in your next home.

Of course, it's not over yet… your bathroom has to keep the same wonderful look until showing are over.

This means every morning before going to work you'll need to do a quick cleaning touch-up to the bath fixtures and counters with disinfecting wipes. Tuck away all your personal items into drawers or cabinets, adjust your towels and floor mats and put the toilet seat down.

Now you're ready for those important buyer showings.

CHAPTER 4
3 IMPROVEMENTS NOT TO DO BEFORE
SELLING YOUR CONDO

It's tempting… install new hardwood floors, add in a new granite countertop, build in new closet organizers, hang new window coverings… all the things you've always wanted to do to your suite.

A typical buyer often has three problems when it comes to doing renovations, and this especially applies to first-time buyers who have no experience whatsoever.

First, the thought of doing any renos scares them because they have no idea what things cost and they almost always estimate the expense as being twice as much or more than it really is. Second, they're often busy, busy people and have no time to do things themselves and third, after paying their down payment and closing costs, they're totally out of money.

So how do you get past these problems when there are some deficiencies in your home? Is it to just swallow a bullet and go ahead and do them regardless of cost?

BUT, hold on, it's not uncommon that those upgrades are quite expensive and won't give you a positive return on your investment. AND, maybe they won't appeal to the buyers anyway!

Sometimes things are better left as they are. Once a client, before he called us, thought he had a great deal on price so he went ahead and installed new hardwood flooring throughout his 1 + den condo suite. All would be good maybe except the colour he chose was not an attractive one.

Turns out it was end-of-the-line stock at a cheap price. It actually turned buyers off the suite and we ended up having to discount the price so a new buyer could install their own.

That's always the danger with costlier fix-ups... the buyer may not like what you've chosen.

Flooring No-No - What we've done successfully in the past with less-than-perfect floors is to get a quote from a couple of hardwood floor suppliers for the cost to supply and install new flooring. Don't do the work... just get a quote. Then we'd market the home with those quotes in hand to demonstrate to buyers what it would actually cost to finish the job.

Sometimes that's enough to get the deal done. Other times we've said... pay us $XXX more for the condo suite and we'll replace the hardwood floors before closing and the buyer gets to pick the colour themselves. This way the purchaser gets the improvement rolled in to their mortgage for only an additional $4.20 per thousand of that cost per month.

Kitchen No-No - It will never give you a $+ return on investment to completely replace kitchen cabinets or install granite counters everywhere to get rid of the laminate version UNLESS your kitchen is one of only a few left in your condominium building that still have the old originals left in them.

As part of our market pricing analysis we'll do for you, we would discuss the features other sold suites had compared to yours. It's only AFTER completing this analysis that we would suggest remedies for your kitchen situation based on your competition.

Closet No-No - Let's say your closets were last upgraded back in the stone age when all people had were a couple of loincloths and storage space in the closet is miniscule. Should you invest in improving them before listing?

There are some terrific companies in TO such as California Closets or Organized Interiors who will do a fantastic job with redoing closets but they're not cheap. Costs will range from $2,000 to $5,000 or more and the results will be spectacular.

So, we have to ask ourselves... would a typical buyer pay that much extra for the enhanced closet space? The practical, cost-effective solution to crappy closet storage would probably be either a Home Depot or Ikea choice of closet organizer which will improve what you have but not cost a whole lot.

Bottom Line - Although improvements like these would certainly make your condo suite more saleable, they probably would not positively influence your bottom line very much and they might hurt it.

IF you were asking me if you should do these kinds of work just after you moved in or when you still had a few years left before you planned to upgrade to a new home, and you would have an opportunity to enjoy these types of improvements yourself, my answer would probably, but not for sure, be totally different.

In those situations, you're not strictly looking at return-on-investment numbers but at personal enjoyment!

Whenever you even just start to have a passing thought about selling, call us over to do a **Room-By-Room Review** for you. It will take 20-30 minutes to do a walk-through and have a coffee and you might end up saving a lot of money.

CHAPTER 5
A FREE SERVICE - GET A ROOM-BY-ROOM REVIEW DONE

Increase Your Home's Value With Simple Cosmetic Fix-ups

Find Out What Repairs And Fix-Ups You SHOULD Be Doing Before Selling

Often people call us up to list their house or condominium and say, "I've just installed brand new granite counter-tops throughout the kitchen" with the intention of course of increasing their home's value.

After taking a look at them, I find they just installed the granite with a not-so-appealing, mis-matched colour and the improvement was wasted!

Or they've stripped off all the shingles and reroofed the entire house when it was only the front porch that needed some repairs.

The problem with that is they now expect to regain that renovation money, and more, which they've spent once it sells.

Rarely will they get back dollar-for-dollar in this situation but more often just 50 cents or less on the dollar spent!

The solution… do ONLY cosmetic repairs which enhance the value (or perception of value) in the eyes of the purchaser.

The Four Critical Principles To Maximizing Your Sale Price

There are four critical principles... **Pricing, Presentation, Promotion and Negotiation**... which, when carried out diligently, ensure that you will get the highest price possible for your house or condo.

The first principle... **Pricing**... should be done in conjunction with your Realtor after looking at recent comparable sales, but the bottom line is that it's your decision to make.

The third and fourth principles, **Promotion and Negotiation**, rest entirely on the Realtor to provide. Quite simply, the better the promotion for your home AND the better negotiator your Realtor is, the HIGHER the sales price you'll get.

Although the responsibility for carrying out the second principle, **Property Presentation**, rests exclusively on the homeowner, it should NOT be done without some coaching from an experienced Realtor who knows what cosmetically-improved features are most likely to attract a buyer and entice them to pay a higher price!

Proper Presentation IS Critical...

After 37+ years of helping homeowners maximize their sales price, we realize why proper presentation of your home really is crucial!

Why is it so important? There are three critical reasons...

First, most buyers have NO experience in fixing up a home, however minor those repairs are. They often can't "see through the dust" as it were to visualize how your home might look once it has been fixed up.

The problem with that is many buyers, through their inexperience, tend to exaggerate the extent of the repairs and attach a 'price tag' which is often 3-4 times what the actual fix-up cost really is.

Therefore they've effectively REDUCED the value of your home in their mind by several thousands of dollars!

Second, quite a few home purchasers are buying with a limited down payment and are 'scraping' their pockets to make up the closing costs.

These buyers just DON'T have the cash to do repairs or fix-ups once they move in.

Third, singles and couples these days are often working many hours in their careers. Once they do get home, the last thing they want to do is pick up a paint brush or a hammer.

This is why COSMETICALLY ENHANCED homes always sell for more money and in a shorter time!

How Do We Advise Our Clients?

We act as valuable consultants and advisors to assist home owners with maximizing their sale price. The **Room-by-Room Review** helps a condominium or house owner prioritize what to do to stage their home for the buyer's eyes, by working on the big things first. The goal… to make your home show better than all the other competitors in the market!

When's the best time to have a Room-By-Room Review done? The earlier that you do your Review prior to your 'ideal' moving date the better.

Why? Most sellers are in the same position as the buyers… working hard and don't have the time to do a lot of work or don't have the skills necessary to do the work. In either case, having a longer cushion of time allows those 'cosmetic only' repairs to be carried out at a more leisurely pace over several weeks or weekends. That cushion of time also allows a bit of time to fit your fix-ups into a handyman's busy schedule.

A typical Room-By-Room Review takes about 20-30 minutes of your time, and you're encouraged to follow along with pen and paper in hand.

We'll do a walk-thru of every interior room and around the exterior to discover the areas in your home where we can suggest cosmetic enhancements which will catch (or avoid catching) the buyer's eye.

We'll create a cosmetic fix-up list that you can either do yourself OR we can even recommend a couple of 'handy-men' contractors who specialize in getting homes ready for sale.

Once you've completed your cosmetic repairs, we have a Home Stager ready to come over and make the final suggestions on how to maximize your selling price.

CHAPTER 6
BRIGHT IDEAS FOR MAKING SUCCESSFUL
LIGHTING CHOICES

Unfortunately, many condo builders simply install the cheapest ceiling fixtures possible when they construct and sell suites so it's up to the owner to make some lighting changes that will enhance the buyer's experience.

Remember, if the buyer can't see it, they're not going to like it.

The first step is to enhance any natural light that's available. Heavy window coverings should be pulled back all the way, shutters should be opened and vertical/horizontal blinds set for maximum light.

In most cases, you should do this day and night if there's a view out your windows. In an ideal world, you'd have blinds that adjust from the bottom up AND from the top down. With those you can manipulate the view so there's privacy but still allow light to come in.

Of course, if your windows are dirty, that doesn't help. Get out on that balcony and clean the windows inside and out, including any balcony railing glass, so the view is crisp and clear. If there's no balcony, at least get the interior side washed.

If there's any furniture blocking the outside view, this is the time to move it away or into storage.

So now that we've got that figured out, let's move on to your electric lighting. First, walk around with pen and paper in hand all the light switches on and make a list of any burnt-out bulbs that need replacing when you go to Home Depot. Sometimes those compact fluorescent high efficiency light bulbs don't throw off much light and may need to be replaced with more conventional ones. You can always put them back in place after the sale is firm.

Do ceiling fixtures have a collection of dust or dead bugs that need a cleanup?

It might be time to consider replacing some ceiling fixtures, especially in the kitchen, bathroom and living room to update them for today's buyers. Good lighting can enhance a room's size and livability and show off specific highlights. Under-cabinet lighting is perfect for enhancing your counter-tops and Ikea offers some inexpensive choices.

Some sort of track lighting is excellent for illuminating various work areas in the kitchen and in hallways. Ideally the fixture would have 3-4 swivel heads with halogen spots which could be focused where you need them. Pendant lighting is terrific to highlight island counters.

I'm definitely not a fan of overhead lighting for the living room or bedroom - it's usually too harsh and makes it hard to read a newspaper or book. Light that flows down from either stand-alone or table lamps is perfect to accentuate seating configurations.

Shop at Ikea or other home supply stores to get fixtures that would be appropriate for your condo suite AND the likely condo buyer demographic that you're aiming for. The expense of new fixtures where needed is very minor compared to today's home values.

Lastly, turn those lights on! Even in the daytime, lights should be on everywhere to accentuate your home's features.

CHAPTER 7
SUCCESSFUL WAYS TO AVOID DREADFUL SCARCITY THINKING

This is a BIG one... getting rid of the accumulation of years of stuff! Sometimes it is piles of books, newspapers and other paraphernalia that have built stacks and other times it is extra furniture or kids toys that have grown in numbers.

Either way, the goal is to slim down, dispose of LOTS of stuff and put items into storage that you will want in your new home.

By creating more 'space' you'll be making your condo suite seem larger than it might be and larger sells. You will also have eliminated a lot of your personal things making it more attractive to the buyer.

Many folks find it easier to begin with clearing out their condo locker, an area where unwanted or little used items often land. Throw away worthless items you can do without and take important bigger items to a storage facility or friend's garage. This will give you some valuable space to put belongings being taken out of your condo suite.

As you collect unnecessary or "disposable" items from your condo de-cluttering, organize them neatly in your locker in preparation for a garage sale.

OK, you've now made some extra locker space available and you've probably rented a storage locker too. Start by taking a critical look at your living room and bedroom(s). What furniture could be thrown away or stored to open up those spaces? Is it extra chairs, a wall unit, a seldom-used end table or desk or maybe an extra bookcase full of miscellaneous books.

Could you get along without that big chest of drawers in your master just until your condo is sold?

Consider getting a second opinion if you're having trouble with the decluttering. Nothing should be considered sacred in this elimination process!

Now that the big stuff has been taken care of, it's time for the smaller ones. Look in all your closets and see what can be thrown away or boxed up now and put in storage in advance of the final move. Eliminate seasonal and seldom-used clothes, old shoe or camera boxes you've been saving and any other items that have been gathering dust in there for some time.

If you've got a wee one or two, a big elimination will be to narrow down the toy choices to three or four. Pack the others away in a clear box in the locker and be prepared to switch the toys out from time to time.

Remember to keep one plastic bin handy to throw all those remaining toys into before you leave for work every day so your home is kept as neat as possible.

The end result will be just a few functional things placed on your kitchen counters and scattered throughout your suite.

Later on, you'll appreciate all the 'elimination' work you've just done. When you are packing up for the final move, you'll now have less to work with.

CHAPTER 8
BE FEARLESS WHEN MAKING PERFECT COLOUR CHOICES

When people first move in to their new home, especially if they've been renting previously, they are highly motivated to go wild and crazy with the colours they choose for walls and trim. They've never before had the opportunity to do up a condo or house exactly the way they've always wanted to.

Rooms of all one colour can sometimes be more peaceful to the eye while different colours on different walls can on occasion add interest and depth to the rooms.

However, when it comes time to sell, sometimes those very personal not-so-neutral colour choices can come back and bite them in the 'you know where' if they don't appeal to a wide variety of buyers.

Unless your condo is very spacious and bright, most wallpapers with large patterns or designs probably won't fit well. Buyers also worry about how difficult it's going to be to remove them after buying.

And, for sure if your walls are showing signs of wear... scratches, peeling, etc... it's definitely time to do a quick paint job of walls and maybe even the trim work over a weekend.

Personal taste is a strange thing and your goal as a successful, profitable seller is to appeal to as broad a range of purchasers as possible.

As a rule, we'd suggest that if you have some out-of-the-ordinary colours on your walls you should repaint them in more neutral shades… off-whites, creams, light greys and so on.

Here are some neutral colours from Home Depot's Behr line of paints our clients have successfully used in the past. Take a look at the colour swatches for Classic Taupe 290E-3, Gallery Taupe ICC-89, Silver Tradition ICC-23 and White 1852 for trim work.

From Benjamin Moore, there's CC 110 Muslin that you can consider.

You can spice up your space with coloured accessories… cushions, small area carpets, a vase of flowers, bed spreads, towels and so on. You get the picture.

Remember though, keep these 'spicing up' items to a minimum so you don't create more clutter in your rooms.

By the way, we have excellent connections with various trades who can come in and quickly take care of some of the handy-man type of jobs you don't have the time or expertise to tackle for yourself… just call, text or email me for a contractor list.

CHAPTER 9
PAY THE HIGHEST ATTENTION TO THIS IMPORTANT ROOM

Along with the bathroom, the kitchen is a very important room to get right when you're selling your condo.

There's often a big difference between the kitchen layouts in suites built back in the 1980's and the 1990's however. They were bigger and many times were an separate room and sometimes had actual space for a small kitchen table.

In the 2000's to the present it's more likely that the kitchen is open to the rest of the suite, sometimes with an island separating it from the living room but quite often is set along one wall and completely open to everything else.

If your suite is one of the earlier ones, your appliances may be somewhat dated. Consider whether they should be replaced with more up-to-date ones. Having 'new stainless appliances' on the MLS listing is certainly an attractive feature.

If your cabinets are in good shape generally, you might consider just simply replacing the cabinet knobs with a more fashionable version to give them a new look.

Many older kitchens will have scratches or worn paint so you'll have to make some repair decisions. You could paint them yourself, hire a professional contractor to do the painting or consider refacing or replacing them entirely.

If you choose to go the do-it-yourself route, be sure to do some research on the correct kind of paint to use for the specific cabinet material you have. You might have to do a bit of fine sanding to remove or minimize any scratches and then prime the cabinetry. Use painter's tape to protect the wall or backsplash tile from paint drips or messes while painting kitchen cabinets. Cover every countertop with a drop cloth. Use a roller or paintbrush to prime the faces of cabinet boxes and drawers and both sides of doors.

There are pros in Toronto whose specialty is painting kitchen and bathroom cabinets. They'll come to your condo, remove all the doors and take them back to their shop for painting. For the cabinet frames, etc they will green tape wherever needed and paint those on site. The cost is roughly $2500-$4000 depending on the kitchen size. One company that does this is PaintCore.ca - get in touch for a quote.

And, as a last resort, you may want to refinish or replace those cabinet doors at the very least or change out the uppers and lowers entirely. This will be the most expensive option but might be necessary if your cabinets have been heavily damaged by wear or water leakage.

Most new condos have snazzy granite countertops but lots of older suites still have the laminate version. If your suite does have the laminate version in good condition, the simplest modernizing fix is to paint it a neutral colour. You can even get granite-looking paint these days from Giani.

First you will need to sand down the surface and wash/wipe away remaining dust. Dry the countertop and then paint with a primer and paint roller. Once that's dried, apply one to two coats of paint and then seal the surface with polyurethane after the paint has dried.

Check at Home Depot or online for the best kinds of paint to use for the type of surface you have.

It's a different story if your counters are full of chips, nicks, gouges etc. You might want to consider installing a new one depending on how bad it is. I'd suggest a laminate version but with a modern look and feel to it since there are some really interesting products out there now.

Now that we've covered the big stuff it's time to think about the nitty-gritty items.

Let's talk plumbing... of course you're going to check under the sinks for any tap or trap leaks and stop any fixture drips by switching out the cylinder or adding a new washer.

An extensive cleaning is essential which includes walls, countertops, floors, sinks, appliances and any counter-top items that are going to remain on display. Don't forget to do the windows, window blinds and light fixtures too.

After you've cleaned and discovered scratches etc which don't come off, maybe consider a quick coat of neutral coloured paint to give everything a fresh look.

Now it's time to set the stage for buyer showings. Keep just a few items on the counters and don't leave any dirty dishes in the sink or out to dry. Swiffer the floor every morning before heading out to work and leave the lights on.

DON'T think of spending anything over a few hundred dollars without me dropping by to do a **Room-By-Room Review.**

I'll give you immediate suggestions on what fix-ups will bring you a higher price and more importantly, what you should **NOT** spend any money on.

CHAPTER 10
ENSURE YOU ANSWER THESE 4 NOT-SO-
SURPRISING BUYER QUESTIONS

There are four questions that every condo buyer will want the answers to and, as the seller, you'll want to know what they are and work out how your suite compares to the rest of the market.

You've heard the first one probably since babyhood... **location, location, location.** A buyer's preference of location will of course be tempered by the price that they can afford.

In an ideal world, a purchaser could walk to work from their 1,500 sf 2-bedroom condo suite that they just paid $200,000 for in downtown Toronto complete with a parking space and a locker with a balcony view of the lake. Nice dream huh?

In reality, people will compromise based on location, price, suite size, building amenities and condition until they find their dream home. Consider how many folks you know who have moved out to the depths of King or Queen West (yes, all that way) or to Mississauga, Yonge and Sheppard or Scarborough to get an affordable condo suite.

How does your condo suite measure up based on its location? Is there TTC or Go Train access nearby? How about walking or bike trails? Does an expressway cruise by just outside your condo window?

Write down all the benefits that living in your specific location could bring to a buyer.

Every buyer also wants to know **how much it's going to cost**. These days with agents under listing homes it's become more difficult to explain to a buyer what the ultimate purchase price would be.

Even if that's the marketing route you want to take, first pay attention to what other condo sellers in your building have recently sold their comparably sized suite for. That's going to become the benchmark for your condo's value in that same market.

Definitely don't overprice it. Even in today's busy seller's market, overpriced listings stay on the market and are avoided by buyers.

You've heard for sure the expression **'First Impressions Sell'**. That definitely applies when selling your condo suite too. Remember that buyers are not just looking at your suite... they're usually seeing 3, 4 or more on any one showing tour.

Your goal is to make your suite shine compared to all the others - follow all the fix-up and staging tips in this book to make that happen. Keep your entry-way clutter free and well-lit so people are impressed when they first walk in. Put some flowers on the kitchen island or in the living room too just to add some fresh colour.

The last question buyers always ask is **'When can I move in?'**. In years past it wasn't unusual for closings to often be 90 or 120 days after the sale date but these days that closing period is more often 30-60 days.

Since many condo buyers are currently renting, they're often keen to stop that waste of money and are motivated to close quickly.

If you're living in the suite yourself, you do have the control in a seller's market so you can designate the closing date that's best for you. However, if you do opt for a longer closing, you need to be aware that you might be eliminating some purchasers from the buyer pool.

If your suite is currently rented, the first consideration is the tenant's lease. When does it expire? If the lease doesn't expire for several months you may have to either sell to another investor who will assume your tenant OR negotiate a buy-out with the tenant whereby they'd agree to leave early. Of course, this tenant-in-place situation will again reduce the number of buyers who would be interested in your suite.

If the tenant is on a month-to-month rental then you'll need to give them an N-11 Notice To Vacate once the buyer's offer has been accepted and is firm. This form requires a 60-day notice from the first day of the next lease period.

As an example, for a tenant who pays their rent on the first of each month, if you're negotiating the offer on March 15th, you'd have to give them their N-11 notice on or before March 31st and the earliest you could get them to vacate would be is by May 30th.

In that situation, I'd suggest not having a closing date before the 7th of June just to make sure that the tenant has left and giving you maybe a day or so for a cleaning person to go in and spruce the place up for the buyer. Thus, the closing period in this example could be almost 3 months.

When you're having a **Seller's Consultation** with your Realtor, that's the best time to discuss all of these variables and how they relate to your condo suite.

CHAPTER 11
11 SUREFIRE WAYS TO GET YOUR CONDO READY FOR SALE

1. Home Prep Isn't Optional

When your boss asks you to meet with him, you immediately drop everything. When your goal is to sell your home, you need to treat your home like your boss! Take action immediately and get working toward your home-selling goal.

2. Clear Your Home, Clear Your Mind

Spending time cleaning and clearing your home of clutter puts a sharper focus on your goal to get the home sold and to move on to the next step in your life. Move things out and you'll be ready to entertain offers for your move-in-ready home.

3. Move It Or Lose It

If you have excess furniture and other belongings clogging up space, buyers will see those items rather than the great features of your home. Be ruthless... pack up anything you don't immediately need and move it neatly into your locker or a rented storage space.

4. Involve Family

Don't expect to do all the pre-selling home prep on your own. Ask your partner, kids and even friends and other family members to assist you in paring down your belongings, moving things to storage, clearing out rooms, deep cleaning, selling items, taking things to a donation site, making small repairs, tackling bigger improvements, etc.

5. Stop Procrastinating

First, list all the things you need to do before you put your home on the market (your Realtor can help you prepare this). Put each task on your calendar with realistic deadlines, adding a day or two extra for dealing with unexpected delays. If you stick to the calendar to-do list, you'll make regular progress and get to your goal of selling your home successfully on your timeline.

6. Fall Out Of Love With Your Home

We understand, it's difficult to separate yourself from your home. It's your special space, and you may have spent a significant amount of time living there, personalizing it for you and your family. Now is the time to step away from your home and treat it like a property, simply a space to be sold. Depersonalize your home by putting away photos, family items and anything that is sentimental. Think of getting your home ready for a magazine shoot with stylish accessories, not personal ones.

7. Grow A Garden Of Colour

Whether you have a yard or not, you can easily create a garden of blooming colour in your home. Look at each room and create colour and interest like a beautiful garden: add colourful accessories that grab attention, place lights in corners to brighten every room, clean windows and open window coverings to make rooms sparkle, arrange furniture to invite visitors to sit down and relax and... add a bouquet of bright flowers to your kitchen counter, dining room table or balcony.

8. Variety Is The Spice Of Your Home's Life

If your house or condo is competing with other homes that are very similar to it, make your home stand out by adding some of these... a bright new doormat, colourful accent pillows on couches and chairs, flashy dinnerware or placemats in dining areas, lush towels in the baths, jazzy new throw rugs, and modern hardware on cabinets. Be sure to shampoo carpeting, polish the flooring and repaint in neutral colours to make your home move-in ready.

9. Don't Skimp On Needed Repairs

If you have repairs to make, get them done. Buyers will notice your home's deficiencies when touring it, and even if they miss things, the buyer's mother-in-law might discover them. If you don't have time to address everything quickly, hire a local handyman before you list your home for sale. It will ensure your home is ready to sell and close!

10. Plan For Your 'Away Time'

Leave your home when a potential buyer is about to arrive for a tour. Take your pets and all other family members with you. You may want to go to a park, store, restaurant or the nearby home of a neighbour, family member or friend or just hang out in the condo lobby. Allow potential buyers to inspect your home on their own, at their own pace, with their agent.

11. Work With A Pro

It's not a surprise that real estate professionals like us can help you sell your home quickly and for the best price. Before you start your selling action plan, consult with us. We can personalize your plan to fit our local real estate market and help save you money too. We'd love to help you get your home sold!

CHAPTER 12
CREATING AN EFFECTIVE BUYER PROFILE FOR YOUR AWESOME CONDO SUITE

One of the more effective ways of marketing your condo suite, especially with today's social media resources is to define who is our most likely buyer.

In simplest terms… are we talking about first-time buyers, parents buying a suite for college-age children, move-up buyers, down-sizers, millennials vs seniors, investors and so on.

Sometimes your condo will be attractive to several of these buyer profiles at the same time which can broaden our buyer pool. Let's discuss a few of them.

First-Time Buyers

In general, the market for smaller condos (bachelor, 1- and 1+den suites) is heavily dominated by first-timers with a smaller portion being condo investors. Depending on if your suite is located close to Ryerson or University of Toronto, then we'd throw in opportunities for parents buying for their college age kids too.

First-timers are excited about become home owners but, because of their inexperience, they are typically more skittish when making a big decision like this and they're fearful of taking on a large monthly mortgage, condo fee and realty tax payment.

A buyer agent representing them would want to make 100% sure they're fully qualified for a mortgage and have maintained an excellent credit rating. As a seller, you'd want some assurances from that buyer agent about this.

As an aside, I've written a book entitled "**Toronto Home Buyer's Financing Guide**" which helps new and even experienced buyers learn more about today's mortgage market. It can be downloaded for free at **HomeBuyersFinancingGuide.com**.

Using the average age of today's first-time buyer, we can target that group on social media platforms and market your specific condo suite to them.

Move-Up Buyers

In the last few years, with the price of semi or detached homes skyrocketing, we've started to see more and more singles and couples, some with small children, moving up from smaller suites and staying within the condominium lifestyle. They're typically in their thirties and are ready to settle down for the next stage of their life.

They're often purchasing suites with larger square footage including one bedroom plus den or two-bedroom suites in buildings that have reasonable but not overwhelming amenities and are walking distance to parks, wee-people schools and public transit.

Specific features that this group considers important include granite counters, stainless appliances, a nice view, a locker and a well-maintained condo building with at least basic amenities like a gym. For some a parking space is crucial while for others it may not be an issue at all.

Down-Sizing Buyers

Downtown Toronto has become a vibrant, exciting place to live in the last few years. Singles and couples with grown children now are often selling their houses and adopting the condominium lifestyle. This group would also include the recently divorced or folks moving back to the city to be close to new grandchildren.

They're loving having a gym to use and being close to walking and biking trails as well as restaurants and some nightlife.

They typically do not buy smaller suites... they're more likely to search out suites with two bedrooms and at least 800 to 1000 square feet or more in size. A parking space is usually necessary as is a storage locker for some of their belongings left over from the bigger home.

Our job as listing Realtors is to match up your condominium suite with the largest appropriate buyer pool possible. Of course, it's not an exact science but paying attention to the possible buyer demographics improves the success ratio of our marketing efforts.

CHAPTER 13
9 DOWNSIZING TIPS TO DE-CLUTTER AND DE-STRESS YOUR MOVE

When singles or families are downsizing, or right-sizing, once their existing long-time home has become too large for them, one of the most difficult parts of the move is deciding on what to eliminate.

In a simple world, you'd just take the opportunity to start over... get rid of everything you have right now, buy all new and have a fresh start.

But of course, it definitely is not that simple for many people. There are memories of all that took place in their home including perhaps the furniture which may have sentimental value or those boxes of books, mementos and family keepsakes.

The move itself may be from a space that has 1,500 to 3,000 sf into a much smaller space in the 600 to 1,200 sf range, depending on whether the new home is a condominium or a senior- or assisted-living facility.

Most down-sizing families are overwhelmed and don't know where to start. In many cases, it falls to family members or professional moving consultants to help with deciding what to take and what to give up and break the process down into manageable tasks.

People will need to look at their belongings in a different way. Typically, 80% of what they own are standard, off-the-shelf items which can easily be replaced while the other 20% are those 'special memories' items that have high monetary or sentimental value.

Once this categorization has been made, the next step is to 'downsize' the quantities of those items... maybe cut back the dining table place settings from 8 to 4 for example.

To help with your downsizing, try and live by these 9 rules...

- Keep open garbage bags for 'giving away', 'throwing away' and 'keeping' handy and, in the first go-around, try to keep the number of bags evenly filled - think of how someone else might appreciate receiving what you're giving up
- Reduce the quantities of everything - plates, glasses, candle sticks, vases, sheets, towels and more - all need to be pared down to much smaller numbers
- Try not to impose some of your items onto family members when they don't have the space or the same memories attached to them
- Donate as much as possible to charities, refugee centres and to new Canadians who may need them
- Pick the easy stuff to start with... do a general decluttering of those piles in corners and on chairs or cabinets which seem to grow by themselves sometimes... and throw LOTS out
- Start using up any canned goods on the shelf and food in your freezer so you won't have to move them
- If you have lots of lead time, commit to 15-30 minutes daily to the 'throwing out' phase - you'll soon see some progress
- Clothes tend to be hard to get rid of. If you haven't worn it in the last few years, it's time to let it go
- Family photos and keepsakes are very difficult to let go of. Consider if they could be digitized and preserved so current and future generations can enjoy them more easily

And as a family member helping with a down-sizing move, remember to be sensitive to your family member's stress at losing what they've had for many years.

If you can, take this as a golden opportunity to record stories around family mementos and photo albums... you'll really appreciate having access to these family voice or video recordings in later years!

CHAPTER 14
IF YOU WERE THE INTERESTED BUYER…

How can we make your home stand out so that buyer will want to make an offer?

Selling your home to get the absolute highest price is all about 'painting' a picture of what it would be like for the buyer to live in your home before they actually do.

Some of that 'painting' is just that… painting walls where needed, decluttering, perhaps rearranging furniture and adding cosmetic touches where necessary.

The other part of 'painting' that picture is in words… getting the buyer excited about living in your condo or house and enjoying the lifestyle that goes along with that.

Part of our Team's marketing is to have you fill in a short questionnaire, in as detailed a way as possible, and tell us what you've enjoyed.

Step into the buyer's shoes and ask yourself **'What is it about your home that would excite you the most?'**

Before you answer this question, consider what you've enjoyed about living in that condominium building and the neighbourhood surrounding it or the community nearby to your house.

Then walk up to your front door and pretend you were a potential buyer. Knock and then enter and tour every room in your home!

It will help if you jot down notes as you think about your neighbourhood and walk through your home. Later, you can pare your list down to a "Top Ten" version and pass it along to us.

Remember... please make your points as detailed as possible to help us 'paint' the picture.

This will help us to market your condo or house better and will give both of us an idea of your home's best-selling features.

Make a list of your 'Top 10' Home And Neighbourhood Features

CHAPTER 15
HOW TO AVOID AN UPCOMING
SHOWING MELTDOWN

What do you do when your Realtor calls and wants to show your condo in say, ½ an hour? I guarantee that this will happen and, of course, we always want to accommodate serious showings, don't we?

Jump for joy first, since someone wants to look at YOUR home, right? Then, panic. As you hang up the phone, you notice that your wee one has been at it again… your condo is CLEAN, it's just not TIDY. Now, what do you do?

Since we all know that the first impression is important, especially if you want to sell your condo for the most money in the shortest time, we have a few tips that will help you quickly hide away "stuff". But first, you must know where the buyers are going to look, and ensure that those places are constantly tidy.

Places that buyers will look include the oven, your closets, kitchen cupboards and drawers and your laundry room. Think about it… these places give them an indication, essentially, of how much storage space there is. If they're overflowing, the buyers will think there just isn't enough room to store their own things, since obviously, you don't have the space.

Don't defeat your efforts by stashing clutter in them at the last minute, no matter how tempting it may be!

Enough of that! What you want to know is… at the last minute, where CAN you hide things?

Under The Bed

With any bed raised off the floor, it's spacious, easy to get to, and no one in their right mind would get down on their hands and knees to look there during their first visit. In addition, kids are probably used to stashing things there anyway, and can help you.

In The Washer And Dryer

Who hasn't seen the commercial where a little kid has stashed a pet in there? We don't recommend putting your pets in there, but clothes and shoes and stuff can easily fit. Although buyers like to look in the laundry, to see the size and neatness, they won't be looking to see if you have things in there. Our caution is to let everyone in the family know that it's a hiding place, and to never start the machines without checking the contents first.

In The Refrigerator

This is risky, you know you are going to be in and out of the fridge – and how embarrassing would it be to have a shoe fall out? On the other hand, if you've just walked in from the grocery, you can certainly stash the entire grocery bag in there, until you're ready to unpack it and put things away neatly.

Behind The Couch

That is, if the couch is against the wall. We all know that things get trapped there anyway, so it could be a quick opportunity to drop a few toys or wayward socks for a quick fix.

In The Trunk Of Your Car

If you have bags lying around, drop them in. Skateboards and roller blades are a hazard anyway, so drop them in too. Nobody has a right to check in your vehicle so take advantage of that fact!

Let me leave you with this quick story. One lady, being a naturally organized person, has her clothes closets organized by colour and like items, linen closets with towels and sheets stacked by size and colour, jars in her kitchen pantry with labels facing the front like a grocery store shelf.

This may seem extreme, but when she showed the house for sale, one buyer told her that he'd buy her home for the state of her closets alone! He believed that if she paid that much attention to a closet, that she must have taken that kind of care with the rest of her home!

CHAPTER 16
5 BEST WAYS TO ABSOLUTELY ENSURE YOUR TENANTED CONDO SUITE SELLS

Owners of investment condos in Toronto have had to have patience while waiting for values to improve but perhaps that time has finally come.

Of course, you've had to deal with several tenants over the period of your ownership and are probably now very familiar with Ontario tenancy laws regarding providing vacant possession of a condo suite.

Tenants who are on leases for a set period of time cannot be forced to leave during the term of their lease unless they agree to cancel their lease. Month-to-month tenants can be given notices to vacate, but only if the condo buyer is moving in themselves and provides at least a 60-day notice.

So, what are some of the most effective ways to guarantee that your tenanted condo will sell?

Suggestions For Lease Clauses

The best way to start is by inserting several clauses into your tenant's lease which would deal with accessing the suite for a future sale and buyer showings. Here is some sample wording that you could use...

(E) TENANTS AGREE that, once they have given their notice to vacate at the end of their lease term (60 days prior to the end of the lease), or the property has been listed for sale, the Landlord will require access on a regular basis for purposes of showing the unit to prospective tenants or buyers. Access will typically be required as follows:

Monday - Friday   Between 10:00 am to 8:30 pm
Saturday and Sunday   Between 11:00 am to 5:00 pm

The tenant will receive confirmation of showing times by either phone call, text message or email sent to the tenant 24 hours prior to the required showing time.

(F) Prior notice shall be given to the exact showing times if different from those times mentioned above. Tenants agree that this shall be their written notice for "Landlord's entry" as required by the Landlord And Tenant Board. TENANTS AGREE that their unit will be kept clean, neat and tidy for all showings, and, if there are dogs on the premises, they will be kept secured in a confined area so that access for showings is not interrupted or prevented.

(G) TENANTS AGREE that, for the 20 business days prior to their move-out date, they will keep their rental dwelling clean and tidy in every way. If this is not done to the satisfaction of the Landlord, Tenants agree that the owner may, at his/her sole option, hire a cleaning person to clean the property and charge the entire cleaning cost to the tenant. If not paid by the tenant, Tenants irrevocably agree that this charge may be deducted from the last month's interest due to the Tenant.

Professional Cleaning May Be Necessary

Even though your tenant's lease probably has a clause requiring the tenant to keep the suite neat and tidy, I've found, after many years of dealing with tenants, that their concept of 'clean' may be different from mine.

I'd suggest you first set a time to visit your suite with your Realtor and look at how it shows as is and then decide as to whether or not a light or serious cleaning is warranted.

Consider Doing Minor Painting And Touch-Ups

At that same visit to your rental suite, take notes and/or photos of other minor fix-ups (marks, scratches, dints, chips, holes etc) that may require some touching up or patching.

Decide whether you can get away with painting over just the patches or should the entire wall be painted. Ideally, you'd have the paint chip colour from the first painting job so you could match things up easily.

How To Ensure The Tenant Vacates When They're Supposed To

There are two scenarios to consider… if your tenant has a lease extending for several months in the future OR if they're on a month-to-month basis now.

Let's first consider the situation where your tenant has a lease for another several months but you want to sell your condo suite now AND the likely buyer is an end-user… someone who wants to move into your suite on their own.

Of course, you should first ask nicely if the tenant would consider moving out early if you got an acceptable offer from a buyer but, if they've just unpacked recently, they're probably not very motivated to move again so soon. You may only attract another investor in this situation.

If you're committed to selling, the only way to make a sale happen to someone who wants to occupy the suite for themselves is to incentivize the tenant and money is the best way to do that.

There are several options… offer free rent for one or two months (the usual closing time anyway), agree to pay their packing/moving costs or put cash in their hand to give them the funds to pay first month's rent at their new place.

With any of those options you want to ensure that they do what they've said they will… i.e. vacate on the date you need the suite empty for the new buyer. The way to do that is to have the tenant sign an Ontario Landlord & Tenant Board N-11 Agreement To Terminate Tenancy form before you put any cash on the table.

Once signed by the tenant and landlord, this form designates an irrevocable date to vacate the premises. Of course, nothing in dealing with tenants is ironclad but if the tenant persists in staying on the premises after the move-out date, you can get an order to have the Sheriff evict the tenant within a reasonably short time.

So, make whatever concessions you need to do with the tenant and then immediately get the Form N-11 signed. Advise your Realtor to set a suggested closing date on the listing about 2 weeks AFTER that move-out date to allow for any unforeseen things coming up with the tenant moving.

Now let's talk about the situation where your tenant is on a month-to-month basis and the buyer wants to purchase your suite for their own use. In your Agreement Of Purchase and Sale you should have a clause authorizing you to give notice to the tenant (Form N-12) to vacate for the buyer's own use.

That form is the Ontario Landlord & Tenant Board Form N-12 - Notice to Terminate the Tenancy at the End of the Term for Landlord's or Purchaser's Own Use.

It applies when a condominium landlord has entered into an agreement of purchase and sale for the property and one of the following people wants to move into the rental unit:
• the purchaser or their spouse,
• the purchaser's child or parent,
• the purchaser's spouse's child or parent,

Since the buyer is not the owner of the condo suite yet, they cannot give this notice... you, the existing landlord, must do this. And of course, you need to have a valid purchase agreement to serve this notice.

The notice period to vacate the suite must be a minimum of 60 days after the first day of the next lease period. For example, if the tenant pays rent on the first of each month and your offer is firm by say the 20th of the month, the vacating date needs to be the last day of the month a full two 'plus' months (approx. 70 days) later.

Ideally you would be communicating with your tenant on a regular basis throughout the sales process to alert them to the possibility they'll have to move and then, once you've got that firm offer in hand, deliver your N-12 notice.

I've often had my sellers offer a smaller incentive to the month-to-month tenant to ensure all requested showings are accommodated and that they keep their suite neat and tidy during the showing period.

It is the kiss of death to a sale if your tenant is hostile and does not allow showings when you need them. You've got several hundreds of thousands of dollars riding on a successful closing... offering a tenant, especially one who's always taken care of their home and paid on time, some compensation for cooperation is a very minor expense in the overall picture.

I always suggest that you take two copies of the form when meeting with the tenant. Give them one copy and then have the tenant sign and date on the back of the second copy that they've received this notice. This will forestall any repercussions later where the tenant might say they didn't receive any notice.

I would also suggest that you have the tenant sign an N-11 Agreement to Terminate Tenancy form to vacate on the same date as on the N-12 notice to make 100% sure that the tenant leaves on or before the agreed-upon date and that your condominium sale isn't threatened.

The buyer's agent would also want copies of all N-11 and N-12 notices delivered and signed as would your lawyer for the sale.

Got Time For A Coffee?

You can see there's a lot involved in selling a tenanted condominium suite and you want to make sure that you don't make any mistakes or missteps along the way.

It's also important to work with a listing agent who understands tenancy laws and who is willing to help and offer advice to make sure you work through the process successfully.

It might be advisable for us to meet for a coffee at your convenience to review this advice.

You can email me at Thomas@LivingInToronto.com and we can get together at a Starbucks near your home or office. If you are outside of Toronto we can set up a time to talk over the phone or online.

CHAPTER 17
KNOW YOU WANT TO SELL BUT DREAD ALL THOSE SHOWINGS?

Sell Your Condo In As Little As 24 hrs - And Laugh To Yourself At How Easy It Was!

If you're going to be selling your condo in the next 6 months, what you might not realize is that the new buyer for your condo is already starting to look for homes.

Every month we have hundreds of calls and emails from people who are just now starting to look for homes and are contacting us for helpful information.

We help these buyers by sending them updates on all the homes that come on the market (and homes that are not quite on the market yet).

That's how we may be able to help you sell your condo for top price in as little as 24 hours - **without even putting it on the market.**

Right now, we have several buyers who are looking for condos in several different neighbourhoods, and we're constantly looking for just the right suite for them. Often, if we can give them a sneak peek at some units that are not yet on the market, we may find a perfect match.

If you'd like me to include your home in our **"Silent Market"**, here's the information we will need from you.

Your contact information

The condo property address

Your home address (if different)

Is there a parking Space?

How about a locker?

What is your EXACT to-the-penny condo maintenance fee?

What's the approximate square footage?

Is the suite owner occupied or rented?

You can fill in these details online at **SilentMarketForCondos.com**, or contact me directly by phone, text or email.

CHAPTER 18
HOW TO MAKE AWESOME DECISIONS WHEN SELLING AND BUYING TOGETHER

Sometimes we forget that most people aren't just a buyer or seller when it comes to real estate. The majority of those in the home buying or home selling process - except for first-time buyers - are doing both at the same time, which can be a bit overwhelming.

It is often a bit of a "chicken or the egg" question for homeowners: whether they should focus on selling their home first and then buying a new place, or buy first and sell once they've secured a new one.

The perceived dilemma is that if you sell first, you might not have anywhere to live while you look for your new home. If you buy first, you might not have money to buy a new home before selling your old home or could be stuck owning two homes.

In both scenarios, the first step is to get pre-approved for a mortgage to know 100% that you can move up to that more expensive home based on your income and the down payment (cash and/or equity from your existing home) that you have available. If you're downsizing, you may not even need a mortgage.

Up until about 8-10 years ago, we always recommended that Toronto home owners sell first and then buy. However, with the busy seller's market we've been in for the last few years, selling first almost guarantees that you'll be living temporarily out of a suitcase in a friend's house, with the in-laws or in an expensive short-term rental.

Why is that? When buyers are going out to purchase a home in today's market, it can almost be a certainty that they will have to put in more than one offer on a home before they get something accepted because of the unfortunate habit that many agents have of under listing homes to encourage multiple offers from buyers.

That results in you going out, looking at several homes, finding one you like and putting in an offer 'next Tuesday' in competition with several other buyers. Odds are that your offer will not be #1 and then you'll have to do that all over again, sometimes as many as four or five times before you're successful and get your offer accepted.

What this means is that you're at the mercy of the market when buying your next home and it's virtually impossible to predict in advance when you'll have a closing date on that new property. It may take a few months before you finally get an offer accepted and you'll need to accommodate the closing date of that seller.

So, we suggest in today's market that you buy first and then sell.

However, you should be prepared for the best and anticipate the chance that one of your first offers gets accepted.

To make that work, we would recommend that you immediately do all the house or condo fix-ups and touch-ups necessary to get you the absolute best price. A great suggestion is for us to come over to your current home and do a Room-By-Room Review to give you recommendations on what work should be done before listing on MLS.

Fix-ups might include tasks such as de-cluttering, painting, removing some furniture, cleaning etc. and giving you some staging ideas.

We would also do as much of our marketing ahead of time as possible… order the floor plans, take our marketing photos and prepare our feature sheets and website / online marketing campaigns in anticipation of you finding the right home. Then, as soon as your purchase is confirmed, we could be on the market without any time lost the very next day.

To speed up the selling of your house, we'd recommend getting a pre-inspection done by a recognized home inspection firm. This way we can present that inspection report to any buyer prospects ahead of them giving us an offer. Another advantage of doing this is that you can do any minor fix-ups that the inspection firm recommends and eliminate them from being buyer concerns.

If you're selling a condominium, the part of the process that takes the longest is getting a Status Certificate from the management company office. Sometimes Toronto condo corporations have those reports available now online. We'd suggest getting everything ready to order that Status the second your offer is accepted so we'd have it available to present to buyer prospects before they give us an offer.

The challenge in this is that we will not know in advance when the closing date might be for your new purchase. The seller might want a long two or three month closing or perhaps they've already purchased something and need as short as a thirty-day closing.

We need to be prepared for all eventualities that might come up.

You can see that there are many factors to consider here and some serious decisions to be made.

Many of our clients have appreciated us dropping by early in the process... often a month or two or more before they wanted to put their home on the market... to discuss all the options and to help them clarify any issues specific to their particular property.

Let's set up a time to meet for a coffee and discuss the best ways for you to move forward with the sale of your property. You can email us directly or set up a Seller Consultation.

CHAPTER 19
GREAT ADVICE WHEN CLOSING DATES DON'T MATCH

If you're buying a new home and selling an existing property at the same time in today's busy market, you'll often not be able to match up the closing dates on both homes so that you move out and move in on the same day.

On the buy side, you should cater to what closing date the seller wants and when selling yourself, you might want to choose an offer that's significantly better for you monetarily but doesn't have the perfect matching closing date as your purchase.

In fact, many clients of ours have chosen to deliberately set the closing dates one to three weeks apart for several reasons.

First and foremost, it's a real pain in the butt to have to move out and move in on the exact same day. You're subject to potential delays at the lawyer's offices to get the keys to your new home (maybe your buyers have sold a home too and their buyer is delayed... and on and on) and with moving companies being late to arrive at your home.

It can become very stressful to match both closing dates although for many years it was the norm.

Lots of times our buyers have wanted to do fix-ups at the new home before they move in... sometimes minor cosmetic repairs and sometimes more major renos. It could be as simple as a fresh coat of paint or as complicated as putting in a new kitchen, bathroom or flooring. Most folks just don't want to live through that dust and disruption if they don't have to.

If you do choose to go this route you'll need to arrange short-term, temporary financing to cover your purchase while you're waiting for your existing home to close and free up your equity from there for your final down payment. This is called **bridge financing**.

Bridge financing is almost always provided by the same lender that you're getting a mortgage from. They'll do that for you because they're getting your long-term mortgage business as well.

Bridges are commonly for one to two weeks but could extend up to four weeks. Beyond that it would be on an exception basis.

So, this is how it works... let's say your purchase closes on the 15th of the month but the sale of your current home closes 14 days later. You'll need a bridge loan for two weeks in this case.

Your lender will supply the funds to purchase the new home, minus your offer deposit and any cash you're throwing in to the purchase and you'll pay interest on that amount... in our example for two weeks. Interest is typically calculated at prime + 3% or 4% which today is roughly 6% to 7%.

The good news is that it's only payable for 14 days so this is not a big number. The convenience of being able to stagger the closings usually far outweighs the few hundred dollars of interest charged.

Now that you own your new home, you can get your renovations done asap and plan the move out from your existing home to be a day or so before its closing date... a far more relaxing scenario for most people.

Of course, don't just assume all this will happen by itself. You'll need to talk to your mortgage lender about bridge financing at the same time as you're arranging the permanent financing on your new home. Make sure you get a commitment in writing from that lender outlining bridge costs so you're all covered.

The biggest stipulation that lenders have when approving bridge financing is that you must have a firm offer in hand for your existing home BEFORE the new home closes. This is critical!

This means you need to be aware of the type of market we're currently in and price your home accordingly so it will sell quickly enough to accommodate your bridge financing goals.

If you'd like to get a better understanding of exactly how bridge financing operates, let's set up a time to meet for a coffee and discuss in detail how the process works and what the costs would most likely be.

You can email us directly or set up a seller consultation at **SellerConsultation.com**.

CHAPTER 20
GET READY… SHOWINGS START TOMORROW 10 AM

Every seller's primary goal is to get the most money possible for their home. After 37+ years helping Toronto sellers and buyers, that is an absolute truth.

Another truth is the more you make your home available for buyer agents and their clients to view the interior, the more interest we can generate and, in all probability, the better price we will get.

I've had some homeowners, and some tenants, want to tightly restrict the showing times for their listing and this always hurts the seller's chance at getting the action they need to sell high.

So why do we want a wide range of showing times? Simple. Buyers work all hours and all shifts of the day and night and are not always available in the optimum six to nine PM Monday to Friday time frame. As a result, they might ask their buyer agents to book showings anytime from early morning to later in the evening.

The showing times I suggest to my seller clients are Monday to Friday from 10 am to 9 pm, Saturdays 10 am to 6 pm and Sundays 11 am to 5 pm. This leaves plenty of time to accommodate almost every buyer showing request.

If we can get a lot of buyers through within a few days to a couple of weeks, and the home is priced right, we're almost guaranteed to get enough interest to generate an offer within that time.

If a client has one or more small children, their bedtime is usually early... from 7 to 8 pm but, if possible, they will often agree to keep the 9 pm showing cutoff time if the buyer agent and their clients are quiet when they're touring the home.

Pets in the home can sometimes be an issue. Cats are usually not a problem since they often hide anyway. Dogs scare some ethnic groups and can be a deterrent to having a relaxed showing, especially if the animal is a large size or noisy. Reptiles? Not so good.

We typically suggest that the seller board their pet short term with other family or friends or in some cases at a dog boarding facility. Since homes are selling fairly quickly in Toronto, this usually doesn't present a big inconvenience for most families.

So How Does The Showing Process Work?

First your agent will ask you how you want to be notified of showings... by voice mail or email and he or she will collect your contact info and pass it on to their real estate office reception desk.

They'll arrange with you to get keys and perhaps a FOB to access your condo suite or house. Typically, keys are left at a concierge desk or in a lockbox ideally on the premises somewhere (lobby, garage or stairwell) for a condo property or in a lockbox attached to or near the front door of a house.

If your condo suite has a parking space and locker, we will provide photos and a location map in our marketing materials to help the buyer visualize what they look like. We'll do the same for showcasing any condominium amenities your building has since they might not be easy for the buyer to access with their buyer agent.

You need to expect that you might get a call at 9:15 am just after you've arrived at work to request a showing for 10 am that same day. Perhaps that buyer agent has contacted his client about your listing and they've finally gotten back to him and they're only available that morning to take a look. This happens more than you might expect.

Your Realtor's office will contact you to request that showing time and then confirm it with the buyer agent.

This means you need to have your home in 'showing order' every single day while your listing is active and expect those early or late day buyer visits.

Before you leave your home each morning, tidy up the sink and kitchen counters, make all beds and put away magazines or toys.

Open any window blinds and turn on a few strategic table lamps to show off rooms for cloudy day or evening visitors. Make your property as bright as possible because most buyers like light-filled homes.

Turn off your television, stereo or radio (or lower it at the very least) during showings. It's less of a distraction for potential buyers and they won't be driven out by the noise!

Unlock any interior doors. Buyers want to see all the rooms and, if they can't, it slows up or stops the buying process.

In an ideal world, you would not be home for the buyer showings. Take a short walk or hang out in your condo lobby with your children and pets during showings. Leave the premises to the buyers or, if that's not possible, let them go through the home on their own without interruption or discussion. Sit yourself down in a room that would be the least appealing to a potential buyer.

If the seller is 'hovering' over the buyer or even sitting in a room the buyer would like to see more of or hang out in, often the prospective purchaser will feel they're intruding and want to hurry up their visit. This is NOT what we want. We'd rather have them linger in your home, sit down on the couch and feel what it's like to live in that space.

From experience, buyers will be very reticent to ask any questions of their buyer agent while the seller is around and the agent might miss an opportunity to address a buyer's specific question or concern if they feel like they need to rush outside.

Remember, don't discuss ANYTHING with the buyer agent! Defer answers to any questions from the buyer agent to us (remind yourself that the buyer agent is working on the buyer's behalf, NOT yours).

Let us be the ones to discuss the selling price, terms, possession and other factors with the buyers or their agents. Our almost four decades of successful years of real estate experience puts us in the best position to be your advocates and bring all negotiations to a satisfactory and profitable conclusion.

We've had clients who've booked a weekend out of town or even a week's vacation when their condo or house went on the market. That way their home stayed in perfect showing order and buyer agent showing access was very open for all times of the day or evening.

Buyer showings are one of the most uncomfortable parts of the selling process. Sellers feel stressed and intruded upon by strangers (all true) but it is a necessary part of the business.

You'll want to hire a professional Realtor to help you through this and all the rest of intricacies of the home selling experience… someone who has the experience and the expertise to make sure you are as stress-free as possible.

CHAPTER 21
TODAY'S MARKET REALITIES - SELLING IN A SELLER'S MARKET

What makes a home sell?

This entire book could be devoted to answering this question. Hopefully the 'getting your home ready for the market' tips and articles you've read before this help to answer some of that question.

But to be as concise as possible, a successful sale requires that you concentrate on five considerations: your price, terms, home condition, location, and market exposure.

Since you can't control all of them, you may have to overcompensate in one or more areas to offset a competitive disadvantage in another.

When is the best time to list a home for sale?

Best time... as soon as you decide to sell it. If you want to get the best price for your home, the key is to give yourself as much time as possible to sell it. More time means that more potential buyers will probably see the home.

This should result in more or better offers. It also gives you time to consider more options if the market is slow or initial interest is low.

Is there any seasonality to the market?

Peak selling seasons vary from year to year in Toronto and weather sometimes has a lot to do with it.

For example, spring and early fall are the prime listing seasons because homes tend to "show" better in those months than they do in the heat of summer or the cold of winter. People like to do their real estate shopping when the weather is pleasant!

But keep in mind that there are also more homes on the market during the prime seasons, so you'll have more competition. So, while there is seasonality to the real estate market, it's not something that should dominate your decision about when to sell your home.

As well, there have been years in Toronto when summer home sales have been robust and the spring or fall selling season was slow.

What about market conditions - price trends, interest rates, and the economy in general? Should they have any bearing on when I list?

Absolutely, but it should be only one part of your decision-making process. It's usually quite difficult to predict what's going to happen in the near or more distant future... even economists who are supposed to understand better than the rest of us are often prone to poor analysis.

Even if you're under no pressure to sell your home, waiting for better market conditions is not likely to increase your profit potential. Condominiums will sell in any kind of market, provided it's effectively marketed and fairly priced.

What should govern your decision more is:
• Your family's needs
• Do you have enough space for your growing family?
• Is affordability an issue or not?
• The positive or negative cash flow monthly if you own an income property

How long will it take to sell my home?

Average listing times vary from 2 to 45 days, according to market conditions in a particular neighbourhood, type of property and price range.

Ask us what the current Toronto Real Estate Board days-on-market (DOM) average on the market is before you sell.

As well, price, terms, condition, location and suite exposure play an even greater role. Selling in any market is easier if you keep time on your side.

Most professionals will tell you that allowing yourself at least 60 to 90 days of listing and closing time will put you in a position to get a better return from their marketing efforts.

What's happening RIGHT NOW in Toronto's market?

To put it into one word... crazy! Average sale prices are increasing for all types of condominiums and houses across Toronto and the GTA.

Since each TREB district has different stats and different rates of appreciation this is a question better answered in person when we meet for a Seller Consultation.

We do send out a monthly email newsletter which closely monitors market conditions.

Subscribe for free at **LivingInToronto.com/Newsletter-Signup/**.

CHAPTER 22
FIND OUT HOW MUCH YOUR TORONTO CONDOMINIUM IS WORTH

The traditional Realtor will often market his service to a home seller by offering to come over to their property and tell them what the value of that house or condo is. He or she will also take this opportunity to demonstrate their marketing plan for that home and how they will be able to sell the home quickly.

The problem with that is the seller typically needs more! They also need tips on how to 'dress their home for success' by making cosmetic improvements and they need to know what their bottom line will be. The seller should be coached on what improvements they should make and most importantly, the fix-ups they shouldn't do because the return on investment won't be there.

The renovations that the homeowner has already invested in also need to be taken into consideration in the pricing. The seller also wants to know what their bottom line will be... how much money they'll net at the end of the day.

What we do is ask a series of questions before we come over for the seller consultation. We want to know what improvements you've done, when you did them and approximate costs, if available.

We'll prepare a Seller Net Sheet showing exactly how much cash you should have in your pocket after the sale. For that, we'll need to know an approximate figure for the balance outstanding on your current mortgage, the current interest rate and the maturity date. With this info, we'll also be able to give you some counselling on future mortgage options if you're moving to a different home.

When we arrive, our first order of business will be to take a tour of your home. We'll make notes on the features of your condo room by room and we'll make suggestions as to cosmetic-only fix-ups you could do to maximize your sale price.

Then we'll sit down at your kitchen table or breakfast bar to find out more about your personal situation and what you'd like most to achieve from the sale of your condo.

We'll bring you up to date on what's been happening in the condo market overall and chat about the various marketing strategies we use to get you the best price.

Then we'll talk about recent condo suite sales that would compare the closest with your unit.

For a condo suite, the most important baseline data we need to know to price it accurately is the exact to-the-penny monthly condo maintenance fee, the direction the unit faces, what upgrades if any you've done since purchasing and whether there is a parking space and/or a locker included. It's also handy to know if the condo maintenance fee changed in the last 90-120 days to be sure we're comparing 'apples-to-apples'.

Of course, we'll need to know all of this before we get together so we can do our pricing research.

We'll then have all the comparable suite sales with us for you to look at. In a slow market, or in a condo building where there haven't been many sales, we'll look at comparable sales going back for several months. In a busy market where there have been lots of sales we'd ideally just look at condos sold in your building within the last 60-90 days.

You'll see what features and upgrades those homes had compared to yours, and how long they were on the market. This will give us the data to be able to provide a value range for your specific home.

Note that I said 'Value Range'. It's impossible to predict exactly to the dollar what any home will sell for. As a result, we will give you a range that your suite will sell within.

In an ideal world with a normal market, we would hit near the top of that range but that doesn't always happen. But, as a seller, you have to expect that the market doesn't always look at your property the same way you do and will make their offers accordingly.

Since you're reading this book, is now the time for you to consider selling your investment or making a move to another home?

If so, you can set up a Seller Consultation with us by going to **SellerConsultation.com** - you'll find out more about the market, get all your questions answered and learn what the present value of your condominium suite is.

CHAPTER 23
NOT SURE HOW TO PRICE YOUR HOME? AVOID MISTAKES WITH THESE TIPS

What is "fair market value" and how do I determine it for my condo?

Simply put, the fair market value of a home is the highest price an informed buyer will pay for it, assuming there is no unusual pressure to complete the purchase. It usually is not the asking price.

To get an estimate of fair market value, call your real estate agent and ask for a Comparative Market Analysis (CMA) of your home. Most agents will provide this service free of any charge or obligation.

The analysis will give you a realistic price for your home based on the most salient points of the local real estate market. It should provide information about recent sales of homes like yours, including how much they sold for and how long they took to sell. The agent's price opinion should be very helpful to determine the right listing price.

What's the difference between fair market value and listing price?

Generally speaking, the owner's listing price is the advertised price of a condominium when it goes on the market. Ideally, it is typically set a maximum of 3 to 5 percent higher than the fair market value.

You can assume that some negotiation will be necessary to reach an agreement with a buyer. However, a home priced too high above fair market value will not get many showings and usually will receive only "bottom-fishing" offers.

Sold Over Asking... what does that mean?

In the last few years we've seen a lot of that happening and it's all manufactured. For the most part, properties are still selling for market value BUT sellers and listing agents are actually listing homes at many tens of thousands of dollars below market value initially in the hopes of generating multiple offers.

For this strategy to work, two things must happen. First, the list price must be at least 10% to 20% below market value to generate that 'bidding war' interest. Second, there must be a set offer date that is most often one week after the listing hits the MLS.

Sellers will commonly list their home on MLS on perhaps a Tuesday and then hold off offers until the following Tuesday evening when they'll review any and all offers.

Sometimes one particular buyer will be very aggressive and want to present an offer prior to that set offer date. The seller has the option to review this 'bully offer' but other agents who've shown your home need to be notified of this offer date change.

There are positives and negatives to this strategy... we can discuss them at a Seller Consultation.

Who can help me determine the right asking price?

Real estate sales agents suggest asking prices for homes based on a variety of information you may not have at your disposal, including recent listing and selling prices of comparably sized condos in your building.

Next, establish clear priorities. If you had to choose, are you more concerned with selling your home quickly, or getting the most money possible? Do you think the agent's suggested listing price is reasonable? What would YOU pay for the suite if you were the buyer?

Someone else - a neighbour, friend or relative - may point out advantages or disadvantages about your condo that you hadn't considered. Third-party views will help you start to think of your home as a commodity with positive and negative selling points.

Then you should decide upon a price that you feel is competitive and consistent with sales of other homes in your area. Toronto's Real Estate Team suggests that YOU select the listing price for your home.

Why shouldn't I ask an outrageous price for my condominium and see if anyone makes an offer?

The biggest impression and most impact a property makes upon buyers and agents is in the first few days or weeks of the listing.

Therefore, the home should be priced correctly and be in 'ready to show' condition from the beginning. Pricing your home accurately is essential!

Typical benefits of proper pricing:

- Faster sale
- Less inconvenience to sellers and their family
- Exposure to more prospects because more showings take place
- Increased Realtor response, which generates greater urgency
- Better response from your listing agent's marketing and promotional efforts, which generate more calls from everywhere
- Attracts more offers and sometimes competitive offers
- Means more money for the sellers.

How flexible should I be about the asking price?

Most buyers also leave room for negotiation when they make an offer. Thus, a certain degree of flexibility is usually called for on the part of both the buyer and the seller.

That 3 to 5 percent window for the listing price above the market value range is always best!

While it is ultimately your decision to accept, or reject an offer for your home, or to present a counter proposal, a good experienced listing agent can be of great assistance to you during the negotiating process.

In fact, negotiation is one of the most valuable skills an agent can offer you. As negotiations proceed -whether in writing, face-to-face, by email or over the phone, your agent should advise you of your options.

Even without such advice, keeping a cool, rational mind-set in what can sometimes be a long, emotionally charged process will usually net you a significantly higher price.

CHAPTER 24
WHO REPRESENTS YOU IN A REAL ESTATE TRANSACTION?

Understanding what type of relationship you have with your Realtor, and the brokerage he or she works for, will help you understand how the negotiation process works when you're selling a home.

When an agent is working on your behalf, an agency relationship is created.

Typically, in Toronto we see three types of agency...

- Listing Agency - A listing agent who works exclusively on the seller's behalf and whose job is to help the seller negotiate to get the best possible price
- Buyer Agency - A buyer agent whose duty is to work on behalf of the buyer, and help them get the best price and offer terms
- Dual Agency - A dual agent (one single agent) who represents both the buyer and the seller and is 'theoretically' neutral in the transaction - he or she listed the home and brought in the buyer

Dual agency also occurs when both the listing agent and the buyer agent work for the same brokerage. In this case, your listing agent still is committed to working on behalf of the seller and the buyer agent, even though they're in the same company, is committed to working for the buyer.

By understanding where each agent's loyalties lie, you'll know what you can and cannot tell them.

An exclusive seller's agent represents only the sellers, not the buyers. If your exclusive seller's agent finds a buyer for your home, I'd suggest he have another agent — maybe even a co-worker from the same brokerage — represent the buyer in your transaction. In some cases, the buyer may have no agent at all. Your exclusive seller's agent is loyal only to you, so it's OK to discuss strategy with him.

Do you want the agent to represent you and only you when you buy a home so that all the information you share with him or her is confidential? Opt for an exclusive buyer's agent.

In Toronto, agents can represent both the buyer and seller. This typically happens when the listing agent finds a buyer themselves for your home, either through an open house or some of their marketing. This is one of the ways dual agency is invoked.

As a dual agent, they seek to bring both sides of the transaction together. Legally, they can't do something that's only good for one and not for the other side.

The agent must disclose the dual agency relationship and both you and the buyer must agree in writing to such dual representation because of the potential for conflicts of interest.

While dual agents have an obligation not to share any confidential information about a client without their permission, as the seller, be sure to inform the listing agent you are working with that the information is confidential. You need to understand that any non-confidential information may be shared with the people on the other side of the transaction.

There's obviously a big increase in potential commission income earned if both seller and buyer are represented by the same agent. Note that I'm not saying it may be an issue if both agents are working for the same company! In my belief that's not the case.

However, it is our Team's philosophy and opinion that, while it's not illegal, we believe it can be a definite conflict of interest for the listing agent to also be personally bringing a buyer to the offer table.

There's just too much temptation to accommodate what the buyer wants when the listing agent has already made a written commitment to work hard on the seller's behalf to get the home owner the best price and offer terms.

A professional Realtor will help you sell faster, get a better price, and guide you through what can be a complex process. So, you'll want to find an agent who suits your needs and who you can trust.

Knowing which type of relationship you want to have with your agent will help you negotiate the best possible agreement.

CHAPTER 25
HOW DO REAL ESTATE AGENTS GET PAID?

Although most likely you'll have a listing agent representing you and a buyer agent who brings in the successful offer, the payment of the total commissions falls to the seller.

Don't think that the buyer is getting away with a big win however. The seller pays minimal closing costs while the buyer will have to pay, among other expenses, both Province of Ontario land transfer tax and, if buying in the City of Toronto, they'll also have to pay city land transfer taxes.

On a $500,000 purchase those taxes alone could range between $6,000 and $12,000 depending on whether they're first-time buyers or not.

Realtor commissions of course are completely negotiable. Historically total real estate sale commissions have ranged between 4% and 6% with a recent average of about 5%. Typically, the commission is split 50-50 between the listing agent working for the seller and the buyer agent working for the purchaser.

In cases where the total commission is 5%, as an incentive for the buyer agent to show your home, it has been common for the listing agent to offer 2.0% or 2.5% to the cooperating or buyer agent.

When an offer comes in, the buyer agent will include a form entitled 'Confirmation Of Cooperation' which lays out how the buyer agent will be compensated upon a successful completion of the agreement.

The buyer will offer a deposit with their offer... usually approximately 5% of the purchase price... and that deposit will go into your listing brokerage's Trust Account for safe keeping until the closing day.

No Realtor will get paid until the sale has closed. Once all the closing documents have been signed and title has been transferred to the buyer AND before your lawyer gives you a bank draft for the proceeds of the sale, he or she will cut a cheque to the listing brokerage for any balance outstanding on the commission (plus HST) due on the sale.

The listing brokerage then deposits the lawyer's funds and pays the buyer agent's portion out of that money.

CHAPTER 26
YOU'LL BE ASKED TO SIGN A LISTING AGREEMENT

There are three main ways to sell any Toronto property...

- On your own without an agent
- List it exclusively with a Realtor but not expose it to the full market
- List it on the MLS (Multiple Listing Service) which makes your condo accessible to all 54,000+ agents in the Toronto Real Estate Board (TREB)

People have their own specific personal reasons for choosing any one of these. For example, we offer a 'Silent Market' for those owners who prefer to go the 'Exclusive' route for a while at least.

However, the vast majority of sellers choose the MLS route because it offers the best chance of getting the highest price so let's talk more about that.

In the Appendix on Page 111, there is a sample 'plain English' TREB listing agreement you can peruse to make yourself familiar with it.

An MLS listing must be signed for a minimum of 60 days after which, if the property is not sold, the listing expires and the owner can choose to either re-list it or take it off the market.

One thing most sellers believe it that, if they're not happy with the performance of their listing agent, they can cancel their listing agreement at any time without questions asked.

Unfortunately, this is not true. The listing agent has, at their own discretion, the choice of keeping the listing 'active' even if the seller wants out and is not allowing any more showings.

It is our philosophy that, if the seller is unhappy, both the seller and my Team are better off to eliminate that negativity and sign the form entitled "Cancellation Of Listing Agreement' thereby releasing the listing and allowing the seller, if they wish, to re-list with another agent.

We are so confident of our expertise and ability to serve the seller well that we offer an '**Easy Exit Listing Cancellation Guarantee'** whereby if the seller is dissatisfied for any reason, they can cancel their listing.

"YOU CAN FIRE US ANYTIME!"
NO HASSLE, EASY EXIT
LISTING CANCELLATION GUARANTEE

Occasionally, Sellers list their homes with agents and regret their decision later... sometimes they realize that their Realtor is less than competent or has mislead them about market values, or that their Realtor has not updated them regularly with feedback about their home.

Here's what you can expect from Toronto's Real Estate Team - Thomas Cook & Partners.

We guarantee that you can **FIRE US** and cancel your Listing Contract **ANYTIME** if you are not satisfied with our service.

No hassles, no conditions, it's easy!

We take away the risk and fear by guaranteeing, IN WRITING, that you can fire us and end your listing with us at any time if you are not satisfied with our service.

We're Confident You Won't Need It...

You can enjoy the caliber of service that you deserve, from Realtors who are confident enough to make this type of guarantee...

We are Realtors who work "**By Referral Only**".

Seller's Name(s)_____

Property Address_____

Signature_____ Date_____

Toronto's Real Estate Team - Thomas Cook & Partners

Sales Representatives @ RE/MAX Hallmark Realty Ltd., Brokerage
785 Queen St E, Toronto ON M4M 1H5
416-465-7850
LivingInToronto.com

CHAPTER 27
ONCE THE LISTING AGREEMENT IS SIGNED, NOW WHAT?

Once the seller has committed to list with an agent, it is the Realtor's responsibility to put their marketing plan into motion.

As you can imagine, with 54,000+ licensed agents in the Toronto Real Estate Board, and many of them new to the business, not all of them have a plan. This is another reason to hire an experienced marketer and negotiator to list your property.

There are many more things that can be done now with the popularity of social media to market homes and work to get the highest price possible. The marketing plan is one of the conversation points that will happen at the Seller Consultation.

Ideally, we meet with a seller early in the process to conduct a Room-By-Room Review to determine what, if any, cosmetic-only fix-ups might be done to enhance the value.

The listing agreement would typically be signed several days before the specific date we want your home to show up on the MLS. That way we would have some advance time to set all our marketing programs in place.

CHAPTER 28
CRITICAL... ORDER THE CONDOMINIUM STATUS CERTIFICATE IMMEDIATELY

The condo Status Certificate give the buyer a snapshot of how well your condo corporation is being run.

It tells us how much money is in the reserve fund, if there are any special assessments contemplated or pending and it includes copies of the building financial statements, budget and the rules and regulations governing the owners and tenants living there.

EVERY condo buyer will want to get a copy of a current Status Certificate (less than 30-60 days old) and have their lawyer review it to make sure they're making a wise purchase.

Normally a buyer's offer will be 'Conditional upon a satisfactory review of the Status Certificate'. Often today, when multiple offers are more commonplace, we want to take any resistance away from buyers bidding on your suite and hopefully giving us a firm offer without conditions.

The best way to do this is to have the Status Certificate already in hand and ready to pass on to the buyer agent and buyer to review before submitting their offer.

The Province of Ontario has mandated that every condo corporation has up to 10 calendar days to deliver the Status Certificate once they've received payment for it. So, in order to have it ready when we put your home on

MLS, you need to order that directly from your condo's management office or online from companies like StatusCertificate.com, CondoControlCentral.com or CondoCafe.com and time it to arrive just as we are starting showings.

The online method is usually faster but costs a bit more... either way the charge is typically between $100 and $150 and it comes to you as a very convenient set of PDF files.

However not every condominium corporation has signed up for this online service so some research will need to be done to see if yours is available from any one of the online sources.

Once you've received the download instructions from the online companies or received the thick package of paper documents from your condo management office, send those off immediately to your Realtor.

They'll make them available to any buyer agents who inquire about your suite.

CHAPTER 29
WE MIGHT SEE THESE TYPICAL CLAUSES IN ANY CONDO OFFER

Although almost any clause can be added to an Agreement of Purchase And Sale, there are several standard clauses we typically encounter that you should know about.

It's best to discuss these with your Realtor ahead of time so there's no misunderstanding or confusion about them when it's time to review an offer (or offers) on the table.

Seller warranty that all appliances, etc are / and will be in good working order on closing...
The Seller represents and warrants that the chattels and fixtures as included in this Agreement of Purchase and Sale will be in good working order and free from all liens and encumbrances on completion. The Parties agree that this representation and warranty shall survive and not merge on completion of this transaction, but apply only to the state of the property at completion of this transaction.

If there's any rental equipment on the premises - common to have heating/cooling systems as rentals...
The following equipment is rented and not included in the Purchase Price. The Buyer agrees to assume the rental contract(s) if assumable: The (item) has a payment of $XX monthly.

If the buyer makes their offer conditional upon a Status Certificate review...

This offer is conditional upon the Buyer's lawyer reviewing the Status Certificate and attachments and finding the Status Certificate and all Attachments satisfactory in the Buyer's Lawyer's sole and absolute discretion. The Seller agrees to request at the Seller's expense, the Status Certificate and attachments within one banking day of acceptance of this Offer.

Unless the buyer gives notice in writing to the Seller personally or in accordance with any other provisions for the delivery of notice in this Agreement of Purchase and Sale or any Schedule thereto within THREE banking days of receipt of the Status Certificate and all attachments, that this condition is fulfilled, this Offer shall be null and void and the deposit shall be returned to the Buyer in full without deduction. This condition is included for the benefit of the Buyer and may be waived at the Buyer's sole option by notice in writing to the Seller as aforesaid within the time stated herein.

If the buyer does NOT include a Status Certificate condition...

Seller represents and warrants that there are no special assessments contemplated or approved by the Condominium Corporation and if any, the Seller will be responsible to pay any such assessments which are known by the Management on or before closing at the Seller's expense. Seller further represents and warrants that there are no outstanding fees or payments due to the corporation and that the unit owner is in 'good standing' with the condo corporation and that no alterations were done to the unit without consent of property management.

Buyer understands and is aware of the risks of purchasing a condominium unit without having reviewed the status certificate and accompanying documentation. Buyer agrees not to hold any party to this agreement, including the listing and cooperating brokerage liable for any damages or discoveries after reviewing the condominium documents.

The sellers agree to provide at the seller's expense a current status certificate and all accompanying documentation, within 10 business after acceptance of this agreement.

Seller warranty that no interior alterations have been done without the corporation's consent...

The Seller represents and warrants that, with respect to the unit, the Condominium Act, Declaration, Bylaws and Rules of the Condominium Corporation have been complied with, and that no improvements, additions, alterations or repairs that require the consent of the Condominium Corporation have been carried out in the said unit, the exclusive use areas or the common elements, unless the required consent has been obtained from the Condominium Corporation. This warranty shall survive and not merge on the completion of this transaction.

If the buyer is moving in prior to the closing date set in the offer...

The Buyer shall be entitled to occupy the property from (insert date) until the date of completion at a monthly fee hereinafter referred to as an occupancy fee. The occupancy fee shall be calculated based on the proportionate share of the common expenses, the estimated realty taxes, and mortgage interest as detailed herein (or designated as Schedule "B" attached to and forming part of this Agreement). Said occupancy fee shall be due and payable on a monthly basis, in advance, commencing on the 1st day of each month following the date of occupancy. Partial charges prior to the 1st day of the initial month shall be pro-rated accordingly. The Buyer further agrees to provide the Seller with post-dated cheques to cover the occupancy cost for a period of twelve months, or such period to be established by the Seller whichever is the lesser.

If the buyer wants a building inspection for the condo unit...

This Offer is conditional upon the inspection of the unit and common elements by a home inspector at the Buyer's own expense and the obtaining of a report satisfactory to the Buyer in the Buyer's sole and absolute discretion. Unless the Buyer gives notice in writing delivered to the Seller personally or in accordance with any other provisions for the delivery of notice in this Agreement of Purchase and Sale or any Schedule thereto not later than 3 business days after acceptance of this offer that this condition is fulfilled, this Offer shall be null and void and the deposit shall be returned to the Buyer in full without deduction. The Seller agrees to co-operate in providing access to the unit for the purpose of this inspection. This condition is included for the benefit of the Buyer and may be waived at the Buyer's sole option by notice in writing to the Seller as aforesaid within the time period stated herein.

It's common for the buyer to ask for further visits after the sale is firm and before closing...
The Buyer shall have the right to inspect the property prior to completion for the purpose of inspection for (e.g., financing, insurance, estimate(s) from contractors(s), final visit etc.) to a maximum of TWO time(s), at a mutually agreed upon time(s). The Seller agrees to provide access to the property for the purpose of the inspection(s).

Asking the seller to provide all keys, fobs etc on closing...
SELLER irrevocably agrees to deliver to buyer on or before closing: two complete sets of keys, building/elevator access cards, garage door openers and fobs for complete access to the condominium unit, the mailbox, the building, parking garage, all common areas and the locker unit for the property purchased. If the Seller fails to provide any key, garage door opener or fob, then the Seller shall immediately pay the Buyer for the actual replacement cost of any such key, access card, garage door opener or fob OR the Buyer shall be given a credit for this amount on the final statement of adjustments.

If there are month-to-month tenants and the buyer wants vacant possession for themselves (need minimum of 60 days' notice from the 1st day of the next lease period)...
The Buyer hereby authorizes and directs the Seller, and the Seller agrees, when this Agreement becomes firm and binding, to give to the tenants the requisite notices under the Residential Tenancies Act, (Notice to End your Tenancy Because the Landlord, a Purchaser or a Family Member Requires the Rental Unit - Form N12) requiring vacant possession of the property for use by the Buyer or the Buyer's immediate family, effective as of [DATE] and the seller agrees to deliver copies of the requisite notices to the Buyer immediately after service of the notices upon the tenant.

Seller acknowledges and agrees that he must provide vacant possession on closing. Seller further agrees to provide Agreement to Terminate Tenancy forms (Agreement to End the Tenancy - Form N11) signed by the existing tenants agreeing to vacate by [DATE] to the Buyer within 7 banking days of removal of all conditions.

Be sure to review these clauses with your listing agent and get an grasp of them before looking at any offers.

CHAPTER 30
WHAT HAPPENS AT THE OFFER PRESENTATION?

First, there are two scenarios... the most common is a single buyer offering to purchase your house or condo. The other is if multiple buyers present offers at the same time, creating a bidding war. Each one of these has some basic similarities and some major differences.

Let's look first at the traditional single buyer situation. The typical offer process takes about two hours of back and forth in the space of a single afternoon or evening. It is the listing agent's responsibility to represent the seller's best interests throughout the process... negotiating hard to get the seller the best possible price.

The listing agent should try and glean from the buyer's agent how much flexibility in price and other terms the purchaser has and then use that knowledge against them in the negotiations. There's that old expression... if you don't ask, you don't get!

Many offers are presented personally with the seller, listing agent and buyer's agent being in attendance although more and more offers now are being done electronically by email.

If we are doing that offer face-to-face, I always try to ensure that the buyer's agent has their clients close at hand... in a coffee shop or nearby restaurant... so we can do our back and forth negotiations quickly and efficiently.

We start off by looking at the buyer's offer, asking some questions of the buyer agent and then asking them to leave us in private while we discuss the pros and cons. We can do one of three things... accept the offer as it is without change, tell them to "skedaddle" with minimal offer changes because they're way off, or most commonly, sign the offer back with changes to price, closing date or other terms in the offer.

We initial any changes we've made to usually one or two copies, sign them all and then give our sign back to the buyer's agent. By the end of the two hours, we've often come to a satisfactory conclusion. If the buyer isn't willing to negotiate up to what we feel is a fair price within that time, we just suggest they go and try to buy another property!

If we're doing the offer presentation electronically, we'll follow this same scenario except initials and signatures on any sign backs are done electronically via the offer software.

There are often one to three conditions in the offer. There could be conditions on arranging satisfactory financing or having a home inspection which are usually satisfied in two to five banking days.

If your property is a condominium, there often is an additional condition upon a satisfactory examination of the Status Certificate. The condition usually gives the seller ten banking days to get the Status Certificate from the condo Corporation and then a further 1-2 business days from receipt to examine it.

I would suggest that you order this as soon as you've listed your condo. The cost is $100-$150. That way we have it on hand as soon as an offer comes in. In a multiple offer situation, potential buyers can review it ahead of time. In the typical situation, we can supply it right away and the buyer then must make a yes-no decision within two business days.

If you don't order the Status Certificate ahead of time, your suite is then essentially off the market for over two weeks while we wait for your Corporation to provide it and for the buyer or his lawyer to review it. If the buyer is not happy with the Status when it does finally arrive, then we've just wasted a lot of potential showing time and we have to start the marketing momentum all over again.

When and why do multiple offers commonly happen?

Frankly this happens predominantly when the property is either priced right at market value or highly underpriced either deliberately or by accident!

It can be risky for the seller to list the home deliberately under market value, so we don't often recommend that.

On occasions where we list at or just above market value however, by luck or skilled marketing on our part (I like that one), we do get multiple offers on our listings. The offer presentation scenario is slightly different here.

We'll first look at each offer independently... I'll call in the buyer's agents one by one, we'll make notes about the pros and cons of each offer and ask the buyer agent if their purchaser has any more flexibility in their price.

Once we've reviewed all of the offers, we'll take some time with you privately to decide what our going-forward strategy should be.

Again, you have multiple choices here. You could decide to accept one offer outright... it clearly is the best one and you're happy with the price and terms.

Or we might send them all back if they fall below your expectations.

And sometimes we'll decide to work with one specific offer if that buyer is able to change one or more points... perhaps price, perhaps closing date or conditions.

The 'doing it electronically' option of course is there if the situation warrants it.

In either of these offer presentation styles, there should be a discussion about the closing dates that the buyers want and see if they fit with what the seller wants.

Another important consideration is the size of the deposits given with the offer(s) and whether that deposit is available immediately in the form of a bank draft (another reason to have a face-to-face presentation) which gives us more confidence in that purchaser's offer.

It often is a more secure decision to accept a firm offer instead of a conditional offer in this situation, even if the conditional offer is a few thousand dollars higher than the firm one.

Why? Because, it's quite possible that buyer could have been caught up in the excitement of the moment (known as the 'auction effect') and have paid some or significantly more than the list price. There's a concern that they might lay awake that night 'overthinking' their decision and get worried about what they've done.

By accepting their conditional offer, you risk it all falling apart if that buyer gets cold feet (buyer's remorse) overnight or a few days later before their condition expires.

CHAPTER 31
5 THINGS YOU NEED TO ASK YOURSELF BEFORE TURNING DOWN A LOW-BALL OFFER

A low-ball offer on your home means that the buyer has offered significantly less than our list price for various reasons. Often the seller feels insulted, but, before you say 'no,' ask yourself the questions below.

Home owners usually have a deep attachment to their condos or houses... it's where they've made memories or perhaps it's the first place where they owned the bricks and mortar or, in the case of a condo, the concrete. And that's normal!

After being in Toronto's real estate market since 1980 I've sometimes seen owners react badly when a low-ball offer comes in and occasionally they're justified in getting angry. However, it's not a good negotiating tactic to just reject that first 'testing us' low-ball offer.

Because that's what it generally is... a TEST.

So, let's put emotion aside (sometimes not easy) and do a bit of analysis.

Is It Really Low-Ball, Or Just Lower Than You'd Hoped?

First, before listing your home, we will have looked at all the comparable sales of homes just like yours to determine what is fair market value. You will have chosen a listing price based on those comparable sales.

Because of this prior price analysis, we'll know right away if the buyer agent and the buyer are being unreasonable.

Next, we should consider what the buyer's strategy really is.

If I was representing you as the buyer for a home AND there were no competing offers, I'd also counsel you to price your first offer lower than the list price to see what flexibility the seller had.

Quite often buyers feel better doing this (and sometimes demand this) so they don't feel they've overpaid for the property.

Of course, on occasion the buyer is just throwing out a ridiculously low offer in the hopes that it might stick.

If we've listed your home at say $500,000 with a real market value range of $475,000 to $490,000 and the buyer came in at $400,000 that would be a true low-ball.

What Should Our Strategy Be... Reject It Or Work With It?

Ideally, although it can be difficult, try not to get emotional about that low offer. Try to put yourself into the position of the buyer and strategize from that point.

The fact that someone did appreciate the features of your home and want to put in an offer is a good thing so let's work from there.

I always counsel the seller to counter that offer rather than just throwing it in the garbage (although you might like to) and then see how they respond. As the saying goes, "It's not about where the buyers start... its where they end up".

My suggestion in this situation is to sign it back with just a slight price drop from our list price. That could be as little as $1,000 or even a few thousand below our list price.

Our goal here is to show that we're willing to negotiate but only with a committed purchaser.

We in turn are then testing the buyers... are they really serious and just trying to test us OR are they being frivolous and playing around?

I always talk to the buyer agent (I can't talk to the buyer directly of course) and tell them they're way lower than where they should be and, if the buyer is serious, bring us a serious offer.

I'll ask the buyer's agent where that low-ball price came from. What listing comparables are they looking at?

The agent might not have the negotiating skills necessary to talk to their buyer about the true market value and I'll offer to help out if I can.

In some situations, I might even share the comparables I used with the buyer's agent to justify the listing price so he or she can show them to their purchaser.

Think About What You REALLY Need

From time to time, sellers have other specific requirements other than just the price. Perhaps getting a specific closing date is more important or having a firm, unconditional offer in place so they can move forward on purchasing or closing on a new property.

As you can see, there are many factors that could influence your decision on how to react to a low-ball offer but the bottom line is, you want to sell your home.

It's always better to negotiate than to reject outright.

CHAPTER 32
WHY SELLER'S REMORSE IS SO COMMON, AND
WHAT TO DO ABOUT IT

**Considering Selling Your Home But Worried You'll Make The
Wrong Decision? Here's How To Cope.**

Almost without exception, every home owner will probably encounter this
phenomenon… you'll feel some sadness when getting your condo ready for
the market and when the offer comes in and you're faced with the reality of
committing to the sale.

If you're an investor, you typically will not have developed an emotional
attachment to the home and will be treating it more specifically on a 'dollars
and cents' basis. If that's who you are, you probably don't have to read the
rest of this chapter.

As a live-in home owner, take some solace in the fact that you're certainly
not alone. Start off by reminding yourself of all the good times ahead.

It's certainly can be scary… it's been your home where you've made
memories and chances are good it's your biggest asset and investment in
your lifetime so far.

When you're selling a home, you're not selling an object the same way as a
car or a lawn mower. There's much more emotion involved.

There is a lot of latent stuff happening. Are you feeling insecure? Are you wondering if you're making the right decision? These are normal reactions to when change is occurring in our lives but when they're intertwined with selling that 'biggest investment', it can sometimes be downright terrifying.

The first hurdle is making the decision to sell and starting to get your home ready for sale. Perhaps there are personal items to dispose of and mementos to give away or store.

You'd think that once the listing documents have been signed and your home is on the MLS that you'd feel better but typically that's not the case.

In my experience the big pangs of regret come when the actual buyer's offer is on the table in front of you and you're being asked to sign the documents. That's when the realization your home is being sold really hits.

I've had clients burst into tears at that moment and it's very understandable considering the anxiety they're feeling.

A good professional agent will realize and understand the stress you're going through and help you make your way forward.

Checking Your Emotions Beforehand Will Help

You can indulge in a bit of rationalization to help you through this... examine the reasons why you're making the move in the first place. What are the flaws to the existing home for your current lifestyle?

It's not that you want to build a hate or dislike for your home but just that you're reminding yourself of why it is that you're moving.

Try beginning to detach yourself from the current home and start building excitement for what's coming next.

Don't deny yourself some time to grieve and think about the memories you've made and the fun times you've had.

If you feel up to it, consider having a 'going away' party and inviting friends and family to help you celebrate the passing of the old and the start of a new set of experiences in your next home.

Don't expect that you won't still experience some sadness... getting past those feelings of seller's remorse isn't easy!

To help get past those seller's remorse feelings, ask yourself what is the best way to start thinking ahead to what the future holds. Keep focused on what's ahead and start actively exploring what's exciting about the new home.

If you're still having problems, try answering the question 'What's going on that you can't let go of?' and 'What's keeping you from moving forward?'.

Uncovering the answers to these questions is the best way to clear your mind and feel better about the move.

Someday in the not too distant future, with new memories in place, you'll start to love the new home just as much.

CHAPTER 33
HOW THE CLOSING PROCESS WORKS - A CHECKLIST OF THE CRITICAL STEPS

Now that you've accepted a buyer's offer, there are still a few offer details that must happen.

First, any conditions that the buyer, or you, have inserted into the offer must be satisfied and either a Waiver or a Notice of Fulfillment must be signed by the relevant party.

Typical buyer conditions could be to arrange financing, have a home inspection, a satisfactory review of the condo Status Certificate or even sometimes conditional on having the offer reviewed by the buyer's lawyer.

Once those have been signed, your sale is now considered to be 'firm and binding'.

The buyer's deposit with their offer - typically about 5% of the purchase price - needs to be delivered almost immediately after offer acceptance to your listing broker's office and deposited into their trust account.

Their offer deposit is credited towards the buyer's total down payment and closing costs. If the buyer doesn't provide that deposit, the sale may be in trouble.

Once all the conditions have been removed and the buyer's deposit is now in the possession of your listing agent's office, you can start to relax a bit.

Your home is sold.

BUT, the fun isn't over just yet. Now your lawyer must close the transaction on your behalf.

What Happens Next...

You now need to choose a lawyer to represent you to close the sale. We always ask 'Do you have a family lawyer that you've used in the past?'.

If not we'll recommend two names, have you contact both of them to see who you feel most comfortable with and then we'll forward all the offer documentation on to them.

Lawyers usually need a minimum of 10 days to two week's notice to close your sale on time, although the most common closing period is typically between 30 to 60 days.

During that closing period, whatever length of time it is, it's going to be busy for you. You'll need to pack, organize a moving truck, reserve your condo elevator for the moving day and change over all the billing addresses for credit cards, your bank, driver's license and so on.

We have a Moving Checklist that we send out to our clients to help keep them organized.

Meanwhile your lawyer gets in touch with your mortgage lender to get a discharge statement. They'll be communicating with the buyer's lawyer to coordinate the closing and transfer of funds.

Finally, with all the loose ends organized, you'll set a time to go and meet with your lawyer in person a day or two before the completion date to sign all the closing documents.

In the event you're not in town for this part, your lawyer can arrange to courier all the paperwork to you and have you sign it with your local attorney and then courier everything back to the Toronto lawyer's office.

On the closing day, the buyer's lawyer wire transfers the balance owed by the purchaser into your lawyer's trust account and then both lawyers go online and electronically transfer the title from your name into the buyer's name. Now the sale is complete.

The seller's lawyer will then cut a cheque to the listing broker's office to pay for any balance of commission due over and above the amount of the deposit already being held by them.

If the listing brokerage is holding a deposit larger than what's owed, the real estate broker's office will cut a cheque to the seller for the overage.

If you're just selling, you will make arrangements for your lawyer to transfer the balance of funds over to your bank account after all closing costs have been paid - see the 'Closing Costs' chapter to see how those are broken down.

If you are purchasing another property at the same time, your lawyer will then, with your permission, take the funds from your sale and apply them to that purchase.

CHAPTER 34
PLANNING A STRESS-FREE MOVE

Let's face it: Moving is NEVER fun! But you can make it a lot less stressful and as hassle- free as possible! For starters, use this guide for general information and the handy checklist to get yourself well organized.

How To Choose A Moving Company...

First, whether your move is local or long distance, choose a properly licensed and bonded company! Although each moving company's rules may vary, generally a local move is considered to be within an 80 km radius of the company's base.

Get referrals from friends or family and call the Canadian Association of Movers for the background of the company you are considering using.

A representative from a moving company may come to your home to explain their services and do a furniture survey. They will probably also point out items that cannot be safely moved or that may need special attention. Afterwards they will send you an estimate of what the cost of your move will be.

Obtain estimates from a couple of moving companies for a comparison of both costs and services that they offer.

Be sure to know what you will be paying for.

Do the costs include loading and unloading? How much does the liability protecting your possessions cover? What happens if something gets damaged? You may find you want extra coverage through paying a higher premium or by making alternative insurance arrangements.

As it's usually less expensive to move between October and June, you should ask if there are any seasonal specials available. Also, try to avoid scheduling your move for the end of the month which is the busiest time for movers. The end of June and the end of August are the absolute busiest for them. Moving companies may also offer cheaper rates at different times of the month.

BTW, before you commit 100% to a moving date, check with your condominium concierge to ensure that the date is open to reserve your moving elevator!

Avoid cash deals with the mover - they most likely don't include declared value protection on your goods, insurance on the trucks for their cargo or workers' compensation. You most likely won't have any recourse if you find broken items after the movers have left.

Book your move as far in advance as possible, even if your closing date is not yet firm. Most movers can be flexible with proper notice.

It is advisable to have your goods packed by the movers. They are professionals and know how to properly ship and handle your belongings. Ask moving companies for the cost of their packing services. It may also affect your moving insurance cost if their company does the packing.

Keep receipts and check the Canada Customs and Revenue Agency website (cra-arc.gc.ca) for what may be tax-deductible, such as moving expenses related to work relocation, or for students.

Be Aware...

A mover who estimates a cost for you far below that of other companies may spell trouble.

Damage to goods packed by you is your responsibility and not the mover's, unless the mover has been negligent in the care of the boxes packed.

Don't sign any documentation without fully understanding it. Don't use, or be very wary of, any mover who sends a flyer or letter through your door once your home sells!

One of our clients a few years ago had a very bad experience with this. A deposit of $500 was paid in advance and then they didn't show up on her moving day. It took her 3 months of chasing to get her deposit back, on top of the stress of having to find another moving company at the 11th hour!

If you are selling your condo and closing on a new property on the same day, be aware that the closing for your new home will almost always happen towards the middle to late afternoon.

If the moving company estimates that it will take 3 hours to load you, plus 1 hour of travel time to your new home, plan to have them start at perhaps 11 am or noon at your current residence. This will avoid them sitting and doing nothing outside your new property while waiting for you to get the keys.

Local VS Long Distance Moves

Costs are calculated based on the number of hours the truck is tied up with your move, multiplied by the hourly for-hire rate based on the number of men required to help. Generally, the hours are based from the time the truck leaves the moving company's premises until the time it returns.

Costs are calculated based on the weight and distance of your shipment. Your shipment will be weighed at a government inspected weigh station.

Storage

If your goods are to be placed into storage owned by the moving company, make sure the costs of storage are explained to you, including loading and unloading fees and the monthly rates.

We pay attention to our clients' needs, and as they become Clients For Life, we hear back from many of them after the move. As a result, we have been told of many highly-recommended professionals related to homeowner's needs, including movers.

Email or call us to get the names and contact information for some companies that our clients have successfully moved with.

CHAPTER 35
CLOSING COSTS FOR THE CONDO SELLER

There's a lot to think about when you're moving, so many of us forget to investigate the various costs associated with closing a deal.

Following is a summary, which was prepared with the assistance of a legal expert, that will give you a guideline for some of the costs you may incur when you are selling your condominium.

Generally, the closing costs associated with a sale are substantially less than those involved in a purchase.

Here's The List...

Real Estate Commissions plus HST

Real estate commissions for agents working in the Toronto area are typically in the range of 4% to 5.5% of the sale price of the property, plus HST.

Legal Fees plus HST

Generally, legal fees will range from $1,000 to $1,400 plus disbursements. The fee may be different if there are one or more mortgages being discharged on the sale.

Mortgage Discharge Fees

Most mortgage companies require a discharge fee ranging between $100 and $250 to reimburse them for their administrative costs.

Additionally, if the mortgage is being discharged prior to its maturity, a lot of mortgages provide that there will be a three-month interest penalty for early discharge, or an interest differential, whichever is greater.

However, in the case of a main-line bank lender, typically mortgages provide a "portability" feature, which means, in effect, that the three-month interest penalty will be waived if the seller transfers their existing mortgage from the home that the seller is selling to the home being purchased.

Status Certificate Costs (applicable to condo owners)

Your condo corporation will charge between $100 to $150 (depending on if you order it directly from the Corporation or get it online) to issue a Status Certificate.

Organize Final Billing Readings

Also remember to tell utility companies, such as your electricity and gas suppliers, the Toronto realty tax department, and your cable/internet provider the date of closing so that all final billings are made and you are no longer responsible for any utility or tax charges after the transaction closes.

How To Estimate Your "Cash In Hand" After You Sell

Here's an easy way to figure out how much money you will likely have in your hand after you sell your home and the deal closes.

SALE PRICE		
Deduct Commissions (4 to 5% of sale price)		
HST on the commission (13%)		
TOTAL Sales Cost		
GROSS CASH IN HAND... before deducting any Financing & Closing Costs===>		
FINANCING & CLOSING COSTS		
First Mortgage Principal Balance		
Discharge Penalty		
Second Mortgage Principal Balance		
Discharge Penalty		
Other Closing Costs (Legals, etc - $800-$1200)		
TOTAL... ALL Mortgages, Discharge Penalties & Closing Costs===>		
NET CASH IN HAND on closing day ===>		

After the listing is signed, we will create an Excel '**Net Cash In Hand**' spreadsheet for you showing what your net would be for a range of selling prices.

CHAPTER 36
CHOOSING THE RIGHT PROFESSIONAL AGENT IS NOT EASY

The Toronto Real Estate Board now has well over 54,000 licensed Realtors registered to work in the GTA area, up from just 28,000 less than 6 years ago.

Of those, 80+% sell less than 5 homes per year and almost 50% don't even sell 2 homes annually. Many of those agents are working at a full-time job for their income and try to do their real estate business on the side, part-time.

There are however a solid core of professional, full-time Realtors who do the majority of the sales in the Toronto MLS. And there's an even smaller group of agents who work with a 'By Referral Only' philosophy and mind-set.

Realtors who work with this philosophy guiding their business have a keen desire to satisfy their client's every need because a clear majority of their business comes from repeat business and referrals from their happy clients. Everything they do in their real estate business is intended to provide excellent advice and counsel and add value to their client relationships.

They also know that, even if you decide not to make a move in real estate right away, that's fine. Those 'By Referral Only' agents are in the business for the long term and they'll be ready when you are – keep this criteria in mind when making the decision for which Realtor is best to represent you.

TO SUMMARIZE...

Has this 'Insider Tips For Getting The Best Price' book been of value to you? We're sure that your answer is "yes!"

What this book really illustrates is the level of service that Toronto's Real Estate Team is willing to offer to ensure that you have the best possible information available to you when we are your Realtors.

Our goal is to help you learn and be able to articulate what your goals and dreams are as they relate to real estate and your family!

When you are thinking about selling your home, picture yourself six months to a year from now. What do you see? What vision do you have of where you want to live? What does your future look like?

Maybe you need more information from us before you can do that projection into the future, such as learning the likely value of your home. We are here to be your real estate information resource centre -- not to rush you into making a rash or quick decision.

You'll find that we'll not pressure you in any way, but don't misinterpret this lack of pressure for lack of interest on our part.

The interest is certainly there and our level of personal involvement will increase when you ask for it... as you come closer to the time for putting your home on the market!

You will get periodic phone calls from us inquiring "How is it going?" or "How can we help you?" but we are patient.

We're in the real estate business for the long term. You know we will always give you super service because we want you to become a 'Client For Life'... not just a client for one transaction.

Once you experience that difference, you won't ever want to talk to another Realtor. There just isn't a need!

We're excited about working with you and helping you out. That's where the fun is for us in this business!

HERE'S THE FREE STUFF YOU CAN GET FROM US

Helping Toronto Home Buyers And Sellers Achieve Their Goals Since 1980

As successful Toronto Realtors helping condo and house buyers and sellers since 1980, we've developed many programs and services to assist people with their real estate needs. Here are some of the plans of action we have designed to help.

Exclusively For Condo Or House SELLERS...

Sometimes people start thinking about selling their property years ahead of time and others jump right in and sell their condo or house within a few days or weeks.

Either way, it makes sense to spend some time learning the right way to sell and avoiding making costly mistakes on one of the biggest sales of their life.

Now that you've read this book, you certainly have a clearer idea of how the entire home selling process works but there are still a few important things you need to do. Our Home Seller University has designed some terrific ways for you to profitably proceed with the sales process.

If you are going to sell your home in the next 1 to 9 months, what you undertake right now can make a difference of thousands of dollars in your sale price, and there are some simple things you can do forthwith to make sure you get "Top-Dollar" when you do sell.

A Quick Way To Find Out What Your Condo Could Be Worth In Today's Market

Before you start making any plans to move up, move down or move out to a rental, you'll need to know a market value price for what your home is worth in today's market.

The best way to do this is to have us complete a FREE "Pin-Point Price" Analysis, where I can take a closer in-person look at your condo and prepare a very specific price for your suite. This price will be more precise than the general range that you can get automatically from any website - and we guarantee in writing to sell your condo at the "Pin-Point Price" or higher in less than 32 days.

Go online to **PinpointPriceAnalysis.com** and fill in your property's specifics… it's that easy

Timeline = 1-12 months before selling

Increase Your Home's Value With Simple Cosmetic Fix-Ups

So, you're happy with the price you could get… what's next?

The absolute best next step is for us to do a FREE "Room-By-Room Review", where I take a 20-minute walk-thru of your condominium and make specific recommendations about which fix-ups or improvements you should (and should not) do to prepare your suite for sale. I will point out the lowest cost, highest return improvements you can make to help sell your condo quickly and for more money.

Set up your Room-By-Room Review at **RoomByRoomReview.com**

Timeline = 1-4 months before selling

Sell Your Condo In As Little As 24 Hours - And Laugh To Yourself At How Easy It Was

Some home owners are sensitive to having a lot of people traipsing through their home or there's some limitation as to their putting the condo on the public MLS system.

If that's you, one solution is to include your condo in our "Silent Market" of condominiums that are not yet on the open market. Because we generate so much buyer interest from our website, Facebook and Google advertising and other proactive marketing, we may be able to find a buyer for your condo without even putting it on the market… saving you both time and money.

Register your condo 'silently' for sale at **SilentMarketForCondos.com**.

Timeline = 1-3 months before deciding to put your condo on the MLS system

Exclusively For CONDO or HOUSE BUYERS...

It's often the same for buyers… sometimes they begin thinking about buying real estate years ahead and others plunge right in and purchase a new condo or house in just a few months.

It certainly is a wise idea to spend some time learning the right way to buy and avoiding making costly mistakes on one of the biggest purchases of their life.

Our Home Buyer University has created several ways for you to improve your knowledge about the home buying process and how Toronto's real estate market works right now.

Enroll in as many of these options as you'd like and be all set to go when the time is right for you. Under each option is a timeline of when ideally, you'd want to be taking advantage of these free services.

Perfect If You're 6-24 Months Away From Buying A Toronto Home

It always pays to get prepared. We've designed a Buyer University educational series with articles either bi-weekly or monthly designed to teach condo and house buyers about the home buying process in Toronto in a systematic way.

Go to **HomeBuyerUniversity.ca** and complete the Buyer University registration.

Timeline = 6-24 months before purchasing

Create A Down Payment Even If You Have Nothing Saved Right Now

Would you like to buy your first Toronto condo or house but don't have a large, or any, down payment saved right now?

Our Free Government Money Report will show you how to grow or add to your down payment if you're a first-time home buyer.

Download it for free at **FreeGovernmentMoneyReport.com.**

Timeline = 6-24 months before purchasing

Home Buying Advice For 1st-Time Or Experienced Buyers

Do you like to understand how something works before committing to it?

The Ultimate Toronto Home Buyer's Guide will take you through the entire home buying process in a comprehensive way and help take away the stress of buying one of the most expensive purchases in your lifetime.

Download the Guide for free at **UltimateHomeBuyersGuide.com.**

Timeline = 3-18 months before purchasing

Get MLS Listings Sent To You Daily Just Like Realtors See

The customized HOMEWatch Program is perfect if you are several months away from seriously starting your home search.

Instead of randomly looking for homes on your own, you'll get information by email on all the new listings that come on the market in any price range and Toronto neighbourhood you choose.

Submit your home buying criteria at **CustomHOMEWatchSearch.com.**

Timeline = 3-12 months before purchasing

Are You Wondering What You Should Do First?

Buying a home can be a confusing enterprise and many people don't know the best place to start. A Starbucks Strategy Session is a casual over-a-coffee conversation where you'll get your big and small questions answered to give you some terrific clarity about what to do next.

Remember, to achieve any goal you need a plan. The Starbucks Strategy Session is the best first step in setting up that plan.

Pick the best date, time and place at **StarbucksStrategySession.com**.

Timeline = 4-16 months before purchasing

Look At Properties Without Needing Your Cheque Book

When most folks are just starting to think about buying a condo or house, they typically don't have an accurate idea of what they can get for the money. They're often worried that they're too far away from the time they want to seriously start looking and don't want to bother an agent to see some homes just for the experience.

The **Market Experience Tour** is designed to help you get a feel for what's out there in the market in the neighbourhoods and price ranges that you feel comfortable with, without you having to worry about bringing your cheque book along.

This Tour is not designed to find your dream home... it provides an opportunity for you to get educated and find out what home styles, layouts and price ranges work best for you well before you're ready to seriously start your home search.

Market Experience Tours happen almost every day of the week... just pick the time, price range and neighbourhoods that suit your lifestyle.

When's the best time for you to check out some neighbourhoods? Choose at **MarketExperienceTour.com**.

Timeline = 4-16 months before purchasing

Avoid Costly Mistakes When Getting Pre-Approved For A Mortgage

Understanding what is involved in arranging the perfect mortgage for your lifestyle is critical when buying a condo or house.

The free Home Buyer's Financing Guide eBook will give you clear advice about how to arrange the right mortgage for you and your family. You'll gain the confidence you need when buying a Toronto home in today's busy seller's market.

You can download the book at **HomeBuyersFinancingGuide.com**.

Timeline = 4-12 months before purchasing

How Large A Mortgage Do You Qualify For?

Often people mistakenly think that going to an online site or having a quick, casual conversation with a bank rep to find out everything they need about getting a mortgage approval but this is absolutely not the case.

The perfect solution to getting a full mortgage pre-approval is to have a private, in-depth conversation with a mortgage professional who will review your personal financial situation and offer options about the best way to move forward.

A typical Mortgage Consultation takes about 20-30 minutes and you'll walk away with a mortgage pre-approval that you can feel confident about.

Set up that very important step at **FullMortgagePreApproval.com**.

Timeline = 3-9 months before purchasing

Here's A Simple Way To Save Time And Money When Starting Your Home Search

OK, so now you're ready to start seriously looking for your new home.

You've read up about how the home buying process works, you've been receiving some targeted listings from various Toronto neighbourhoods, you've been on a few (or several) Market Experience Tours to get a feel for the current market and your full mortgage pre-approval is in place.

The next big step is to meet up with your buyer agent for a comprehensive, in-office or online Buyer Consultation so you're fully prepared when you hit the bricks looking for that perfect condo or house.

A Buyer Consultation with an experienced, professional agent should take approximately 60 minutes… there's a lot to cover and understand and you don't want to make any mistakes or get stressed out in the process.

Arrange to meet with us for a very informative consultation at **BuyerConsultation.com**.

Timeline = 3-5 months before purchasing

Here's How To Get In Touch...

Thomas Cook
Real Estate Sales Representative @ RE/MAX Hallmark Realty Ltd Brokerage

Mobile | 647-962-1650
Office | 416-465-7850

LivingInToronto.com
Direct | Thomas@LivingInToronto.com

Author | Ultimate Home Buyer's Guide, the Home Buyer's Financing Guide, the Free Government Money Report and other informative real estate publications and reports

Experience | | Thousands of homes sold since 1980
Professional Designations | | ABR, SRES
Awards | | RE/MAX's 2ND highest award - Circle Of Legends
Charity Support | | Over $115,000 contributed to the Toronto Sick Kids Hospital
Speaker & Agent Coach | | Delivered seminars and presentations to the public and Realtors about buying and selling real estate since 1995

APPENDIX

Listing Agreement – Plain English version

Working With A Realtor – Plain English version

You Absolutely, Positively Need To Know What These Mean

    Real Estate Terms You Should Know
    Mortgage Terms You Should Know

LISTING AGREEMENT – PLAIN ENGLISH VERSION

Full PDF document can be downloaded at…
http://tinyurl.com/Listing-Agreement-English

OREA Ontario Real Estate Association

Form 200
for use in the Province of Ontario

Listing Agreement
Seller Representation Agreement
Authority to Offer for Sale

Toronto Real Estate Board

GENERAL USE: This Form is a contract between a Seller and a real estate company that gives the real estate company permission to act on the Seller's behalf when they offer their home for sale in the open market. A written agreement is necessary in order to secure commission and to ensure compliance with the REBBA Code of Ethics.

This section of the Agreement identifies the parties involved and specifies the time period for the contract. If the time period is greater than six months then the Real Estate and Business Brokers Act and the Real Estate Council of Ontario require that the Seller(s) initial in the oval beside the bracket. There is also a statement in the form of a representation or warranty stating that the Sellers are party to another contract whether a Listing or an agreement to pay commission.

This is a Multiple Listing Service® Agreement ( ) (Seller's Initials) **OR** **Exclusive Listing Agreement** **EXCLUSIVE** ( ) (Seller's Initials)

BETWEEN:

BROKERAGE: .... (the "Listing Brokerage") Tel.No. (..........)....................................

SELLER(S): .... (the "Seller")

In consideration of the Listing Brokerage listing the real property **for sale** known as.. (the "Property")

the Seller hereby gives the Listing Brokerage the **exclusive and irrevocable** right to act as the Seller's agent, **commencing** at 12:01 a.m. on the .... day

of ...., 20........, **until** 11:59 p.m. on the .... day of ...., 20........ [the "Listing Period"],

{ Seller acknowledges that the length of the Listing Period is negotiable between the Seller and the Listing Brokerage and, if an MLS® listing, may be subject to minimum requirements of the real estate board, however, in accordance with the Real Estate and Business Brokers Act (2002), **if the Listing Period exceeds six months, the Listing Brokerage must obtain the Seller's initials.** } ( ) (Seller's Initials)

to offer the Property **for sale** at a price of: Dollars (CDN$) ....

.... Dollars

and upon the terms particularly set out herein, or at such other price and/or terms acceptable to the Seller. It is understood that the price and/or terms set out herein are at the Seller's personal request, after full discussion with the Listing Brokerage's representative regarding potential market value of the Property.

The Seller hereby represents and warrants that the Seller is not a party to any other listing agreement for the Property or agreement to pay commission to any other real estate brokerage for the sale of the Property.

1. DEFINITIONS AND INTERPRETATIONS: This paragraph clarifies the terms used in the Agreement and defines Buyer and Seller as they are referred to in the document.

1. **DEFINITIONS AND INTERPRETATIONS:** For the purposes of this Agreement ["Authority" or "Agreement"]: "Seller" includes vendor, a "buyer" includes a purchaser, or a prospective purchaser. A "real estate board" includes a real estate association. A purchase shall be deemed to include the entering into of any agreement to exchange, or the obtaining of an option to purchase which is subsequently exercised. Commission shall be deemed to include other remuneration. This Agreement shall be read with all changes of gender or number required by the context. For purposes of this Agreement, anyone introduced to or shown the Property shall be deemed to include any spouse, heirs, executors, administrators, successors, assigns, related corporations and affiliated corporations. Related corporations or affiliated corporations shall include any corporation where one half or a majority of the shareholders, directors or officers of the related or affiliated corporation are the same person(s) as the shareholders, directors, or officers of the corporation introduced to or shown the Property.

2. COMMISSION: An important section of the Agreement as it sets out fee that will be paid to real estate company. It also authorizes the real estate company to cooperate with any other real estate companies in order to sell the property. This section details how the commission paid to the Listing real estate company will be shared with the cooperating real estate company. In addition there is a period after the expiry of the Agreement where the real estate company would be entitled to commission if the Buyer was introduced to or shown the property during the contract period. This is the "holdover period".

2. **COMMISSION:** In consideration of the Listing Brokerage listing the Property, the Seller agrees to pay the Listing Brokerage a commission of ....% of the sale price of the Property or .... for any valid offer to purchase the Property from any source whatsoever obtained during the Listing Period and on the terms and conditions set out in this Agreement **OR** such other terms and conditions as the Seller may accept. The Seller authorizes the Listing Brokerage to co-operate with any

other registered real estate brokerage (co-operating brokerage) to offer to pay the co-operating brokerage a commission of.............% of the sale price

INITIALS OF LISTING BROKERAGE: ( )   **INITIALS OF SELLER(S):** ( )

WORKING WITH A REALTOR – PLAIN ENGLISH VERSION

Full PDF document can be downloaded at…
http://tinyurl.com/WorkingWithRealtor-English

OREA Ontario Real Estate Association · **Working with a REALTOR®** · **Toronto Real Estate Board**

Form 810
for use in the Province of Ontario

GENERAL USE: This form is required under Section 10 of the Code of Ethics to fulfill the requirements of Information Before Agreements.

The first section of this form highlights that a contract for real estate services is with the brokerage. Each REALTOR® is employed by the brokerage to provide the services of the brokerage. The brokerage falls under the responsibility of the Broker of Record. Also important to note that the consumer is entitled to know the different types of service relationships that are available.

The REALTOR® Consumer Relationship

In Ontario, the real estate profession is governed by the Real Estate and Business Brokers Act, 2002, and Associated Regulations (REBBA 2002 or Act), administered by the Real Estate Council of Ontario (RECO). All Ontario REALTORS® are registered under the Act and governed by its provisions. REBBA 2002 is consumer protection legislation, regulating the conduct of real estate brokerages and their salespeople/brokers. The Act provides consumer protection in the form of deposit insurance and requires every salesperson/broker to carry errors & omission (E&O) insurance.

When you choose to use the services of a REALTOR®, it is important to understand that this individual works on behalf of a real estate brokerage, usually a company. The brokerage is operated by a Broker of Record, who has the ultimate responsibility for the employees registered with the brokerage. When you sign a contract, it is with the brokerage, not with the salesperson/broker employee.

The Act also requires that the brokerage (usually through its REALTORS®) explain the types of service alternatives available to consumers and the services the brokerage will be providing. The brokerage must document the relationship being created between the brokerage and the consumer, and submit it to the consumer for his/her approval and signature. The most common relationships are "client" and "customer", but other options may be available in the marketplace.

The first discussion in this form is about a client relationship. It is important to note that this is the highest level of relationship between a REALTOR® and a consumer. There are duties which the law states are mandatory to a client called fiduciary duties. The "client" arrangement is created through a representation agreement. Clients can be Sellers or Buyers. The representation agreements can come in the form of a Listing Agreement or Buyer Representation Agreement. While in a client relationship the brokerage must protect the interests of the client and not disclose confidential information there is still an obligation to treat all other parties to the transaction with fairness, honesty and integrity.

Client

A "client" relationship creates the highest form of obligation for a REALTOR® to a consumer. The brokerage and its salespeople/brokers have a fiduciary (legal) relationship with the client and represent the interests of the client in a real estate transaction. The REALTOR® will establish this relationship with the use of a representation agreement, called a Listing Agreement with the seller and a Buyer Representation Agreement with the buyer. The agreement contains an explanation of the services the brokerage will be providing, the fee arrangement for those services, the obligations the client will have under the agreement, and the expiry date of the agreement. Ensure that you have read and fully understand any such agreement before you sign the document.

Once a brokerage and a consumer enter into a client relationship, the brokerage must protect the interests of the client and do what is best for the client. A brokerage must strive for the benefit of the client and must not disclose a client's confidential information to others. Under the Act, the brokerage must also make reasonable efforts to determine any material facts relating to the transaction that would be of interest to the client and must inform the client of those facts. Although they are representing the interests of their client, they must still treat all parties to the transaction with fairness, honesty, and integrity.

There will be instances where a consumer does not wish to have a client relationship with the brokerage. In those instances the consumer can have a customer relationship. The REALTOR® is still required to treat the customer with honesty, fairness and integrity but the services will be on a restricted level.

Customer

A buyer or seller may not wish to be under contract as a client with the brokerage but would rather be treated as a customer. A REALTOR® is obligated to treat every person in a real estate transaction with honesty, fairness, and integrity, but unlike a client, provides a customer with a restricted level of service. Services provided to a customer may include showing the property or properties, drafting the offer, presenting the offer, etc. Brokerages use a Customer Service Agreement to document the services they are providing to a buyer or seller customer.

Under the Act, the REALTOR® has disclosure obligations to a customer and must disclose material facts known to the brokerage that relate to the transaction.

It is possible that the brokerage will be representing more than one client on a transaction or where there is more than one offer on a property. Where the brokerage represents more than one client on a transaction this is called multiple representation. There are mandatory requirements that have to be fulfilled in these circumstances. All the clients to the transaction must confirm in writing that they acknowledge, understand and consent to the multiple representation aspect of the relationship.

What Happens When...

Buyer(s) and the seller(s) are sometimes under contract with the same brokerage when properties are being shown or an offer is being contemplated. There can be instances when there is more than one offer on a property and more than one buyer and seller are under a representation agreement with the same brokerage. This situation is referred to as multiple representation. Under the Act, the REALTORS® and their brokerage must make sure all buyers, sellers, and their REALTORS® confirm in writing that they acknowledge, understand, and consent to the situation before their offer is made. REALTORS® typically use what is called a Confirmation of Co-operation and Representation form to document this situation.

Offer negotiations may become stressful, so if you have any questions when reference is made to multiple representation or multiple offers, please ask your REALTOR® for an explanation.

REALTORS® must disclose facts that may affect a reasonable buying or selling decision. In order to ensure that the REALTOR® adheres to their buyer's or seller's best interest it is important for buyers and sellers to discuss their needs and wants and any issues that would affect their decision to buy or sell. Hopefully, this would avoid any misunderstandings or unpleasant surprises. Further, it is important for consumers to read and understand every contract before that contract becomes finalized.

Critical Information

REALTORS® are obligated to disclose facts that may affect a buying or selling decision. It may be difficult for a REALTOR® to judge what facts are important. They also may not be in a position to know a fact. You should communicate to your REALTOR® what information and facts about a property are important to you in making a buying or selling decision, and document this information to avoid any misunderstandings and/or unpleasant surprises.

Similarly, services that are important to you and are to be performed by the brokerage, or promises that have been made to you, should be documented in your contract with the brokerage and its salesperson/broker.

To ensure the best possible real estate experience, make sure all your questions are answered by your REALTOR®. You should read and understand every contract before you finalize it.

Form 810 New 2015 **Page 2 of 3**

YOU ABSOLUTELY, POSITIVELY NEED TO KNOW WHAT THESE MEAN

As you're considering selling your home in today's busy market, even though you're already a home owner, you might want to re-familiarize yourself with the terms of the business so that you will be speaking the same "language" as the real estate and mortgage financing professionals in the field!

Real Estate Terms You Should Know

Real Estate:
Most commonly includes the sale of real property such as houses, condominiums and commercial property but also includes the rental of real estate and the sale of businesses.

Real Estate Broker or Salesperson:
An intermediary between the buyer and seller who is licensed by the Province of Ontario to carry out such activities.

Listing Agent:
This is the Realtor who is acting on behalf of the seller in the transaction. His or her goal is to get the highest price and best terms for the seller.

Buyer Agent:
This is the Realtor who has signed a Buyer Representation Agreement (BRA) with the buyer and who is now representing the best interests of the buyer. Their goal is to get the lowest price and best terms for the buyer.

Dual Agency:

There are two distinctions to dual agency. The first is where one agent who starts off as the listing agent is also trying to represent the buyer in the transaction and collect both halves of the commission.

Our Team considers this to be a direct conflict of interest and, if we are representing the seller as their listing agent, we will not also try to represent the buyer at the same time.

The other occurrence of 'dual agency' happens when the buyer agent who brings an offer on a condo or house where I'm the listing agent is also an agent at RE/MAX Hallmark where I work.

Since that agent will have no knowledge of any of my discussions with the seller (Hallmark has over 1100 agents now) there is no conflict… I'm going to work hard to get the seller the best price and the buyer agent is going to do the same for their buyer client.

Similarly, if I'm the buyer agent presenting an offer to a Hallmark listing agent, I know he or she is working on behalf of the seller and they know I'm working on the buyer's behalf… no conflict!!

Real Property:

The combination of the tangible and intangible attributes of land and improvements. Value-wise, it is the sum of the value of the real estate, considered as land and structure.

Fair Market Value:

The highest price, in terms of money, that the property will bring to a willing seller if exposed for sale on the open market while allowing a reasonable time to find a willing buyer, buying with the knowledge of all the uses, and with neither party acting under necessity, compulsion or peculiar and special circumstances.

Assessed Value:

A valuation placed upon property by the Province, as a basis for municipal taxation. This is NOT the same as market value and, so far in Ontario, although we have 'Market Value Assessment', the assessed value is NOT 100% accurate as to current market value.

Appraisal:

The act or process of estimating value. This appraisal is done for mortgage-lending purposes and may not necessarily match the sale price of the property.

Salesperson (Sales Representative):

An employee of a broker authorized to trade in Real Estate ... your agent.

Agreement of Purchase and Sale (Offer to Purchase):

A contract by which one party agrees to sell and another agrees to purchase. The contract may be firm (no conditions attached), or conditional (certain conditions must be fulfilled).

Deposit:

Payment of money or other valuable consideration as pledge for fulfilment of contract; given as a "piece of paper" when the offer is signed and converted to a bank draft or other form of payment once the offer has been accepted.

In a busy market to make their offer more attractive to the seller, often the buyer provides a bank draft as their deposit at the same time as their offer is presented.

The deposit in Toronto is typically 5 - 7% of the purchase price.

Down Payment:

The down payment is the total amount of money that the buyer is paying for the property and is then financing the balance of the purchase price as a mortgage. The down payment includes the buyer's deposit with their offer.

For example, a purchaser might have 20% of the purchase price as their down payment of which 5% is their deposit with the offer. Then on closing, they pay the balance of their down payment (another 15%) plus their closing costs.

Irrevocable:

Incapable of being recalled or revoked; unchangeable, unalterable.

Irrevocable Date:

The date that the offer, from either buyer or seller, is good until. It is typically "same day the offer is signed," or up to 48 hours after the signing (or counter-signing) date.

When the buyer signs their offer, they will make it 'irrevocable' to the seller for a specific period... say 11:00 pm tonight or 3:00 pm tomorrow. Similarly, when a seller counter-signs that offer, they could change the irrevocable date and time.

Condition:
A condition in a contract calling for the happening of some event, or the performance of some act, before the agreement becomes firm and binding for all parties.

Conditional Offer:
An Agreement of Purchase and Sale may be subject to specific conditions. These conditions could be arranging a mortgage or a home inspection, or the inspection of a condominium Status Certificate. There is always a time limit stipulated within which the specified conditions must be met.

Firm Offer:
Very common in today's busy Toronto market, to make their offer more attractive to the seller, they will remove all conditions from their offer so that, once the seller accepts it, the deal is done and the sale is 'firm and binding'.

Holding Off Offers:
Starting a few years ago, some agents have taken to advising their sellers to underlist their home by a significant amount (often by 10-20%) and then to start showings but not accept offers for typically 7 days.

This is done in the hope of creating an auction effect where several buyers will bid against each other and end up paying the seller above market value.

There are pros and cons to doing this which we can review during our Seller Consultation.

Bully Offer:
So, you've decided to hold off offers for a week BUT a buyer agent calls and says they have an offer that is irrevocable only to tonight at 11:00 pm. If you refuse to see it, the buyers are going elsewhere. This is a bully offer.

Again, there are pros and cons to accepting that bully offer which we can discuss.

Sealed and Delivered:
A term indicating that a seller has received adequate consideration as evidenced by his voluntary delivery. The word "sealed" adds more strength, since under old conveyancing law an official seal was used as a substitute for consideration.

Home Inspection:
The examination of the house or condominium by an expert selected by the buyer. It's not common to have an inspection done for a high-rise condo suite but, if the buyer has some concerns, it can be asked for and arranged.

Closing Date:
The date specified in the Agreement of Purchase and Sale when the buyer is to deliver the balance of money due and the seller is to deliver a duly executed deed and vacant possession of the property.

Permanent Fixtures:
Permanent improvements to property that may not be removed upon the sale of the property (furnace, central air conditioning, pool, windows, etc).

Chattels:
Personal property that is tangible and moveable, such as appliances, blinds, light fixtures, etc.

Encumbrances:
Outstanding claim or lien recorded against property, or any legal right to the use of the property, by another person who is not the owner. Recently we've seen that builders have installed rental furnaces into condo suites.

These must be declared by the seller and unfortunately, they must be accepted by the buyer (usually the pay-out to the rental company is so high that it's better to just accept the rental situation).

Adjustments:
Adjustments may be property taxes (either unpaid or paid in advance), electricity, gas or other fuel, condo fees or mortgage interest already paid out for future service. These must be pro-rated and be credited on closing to the appropriate side of the transaction. This can involve an expenditure of several hundred dollars payable on the closing date when the sale is completed.

Statement of Adjustments:
A statement of the financial breakdown of the transaction prepared by the solicitor for the seller setting out, in balance sheet form, the credits to the seller (e.g. purchase price, prepaid taxes, prepaid insurance, etc.) and the credits to the buyer (e.g. deposits, arrears in taxes prior to the date of closing) and the balance due on closing.

Closing Costs:
These will include such items as Province of Ontario Land Transfer Tax, City of Toronto Land Transfer Tax, legal fees and disbursements, HST on high-ratio mortgage insurance premium, appraisal cost, Status Certificate fee, etc.

Our Team will prepare a Closing Cost Estimate spreadsheet at the Starbucks Strategy Session or at the Buyer Consultation to give you an excellent idea of how much money you need to set aside for these expenses.

Survey:
The accurate mathematical measurement of land and buildings thereon, made with the aid of instruments by a licensed land surveyor. They show the legal boundaries of the property, the location of any buildings on the lot plus measurements. Surveys are not done for condominium suites.

Title:
The means of evidence by which the owner of land has lawful ownership thereof.

Buydown:
Although typically rare these days with our low interest rates, the seller effectively lowers the rate of interest of a mortgage for the buyer by prepaying a portion of the interest on his own existing mortgage, or on a mortgage arranged by the buyer.

Canada Mortgage and Housing Corporation (CMHC):
The federal CMHC is the Canadian crown corporation that administers the National Housing Act. CMHC services include providing housing information and assistance to consumers and insuring home purchase loans for lenders.

See below the definitions of conventional and high-ratio mortgages.

Deed:

The final document prepared by a lawyer or notary to be signed by the seller and buyer transferring ownership. This document is then registered against the property as evidence of ownership.

Deeds are now prepared and registered electronically in Toronto by the buyer's lawyer in co-operation with the seller's lawyer.

Mortgage Discharge:

The removal of all mortgages and other encumbrances typically at the time of sale by paying off all outstanding liens registered against the title of the property.

Easement and Right-Of-Way:

The right acquired for access to, or over another person's land for a specific purpose, such as for a driveway or public utilities.

A semi-detached house might have a 'mutual drive' meaning that the lot line goes close to the centre of the space between the two houses but each home owner has a right-of-way over the other person's half of the driveway to access the back yard.

Encroachment:

The unauthorized extension of boundaries of land, such as when a homeowner puts up a fence or perhaps a utility shed over the lot line and "takes over" some of a neighbour's property.

Holdback:

An amount of money withheld by the lender during the progress of construction of a new house or major renovation to ensure that construction is satisfactory at every stage. The amount of the holdback is generally equivalent to the estimated cost to complete construction.

Home Insurance:

Before the sale transaction can be closed, the buyer must have fire and liability insurance arranged and in effect. A certificate from the insurance company (called a 'binder') will be required by your lawyer at the closing as proof that you have that coverage.

This applies to condo purchases as well although it's much cheaper. Condo buildings have their own insurance so the owner's policy must only cover the contents, liability plus enough coverage to pay for the replacement of any upgrades that have been done to the unit over and above what the original builder provided.

Owner's Net Equity:

The difference between the price for which a property could be sold and the total debts (mortgages or liens) registered against it.

Option Agreement:

A document stipulating that, in exchange for a deposit, a specified individual is to be given first chance or option to buy a property within a specified period. If the option-holder does not buy within the specified time, he loses his deposit.

Power of Sale:

The right of a bank or trust company to force the sale of the property without judicial proceedings, should the owner default on their mortgage payments.

Prospect:

A potential buyer or customer.

Commission:

Percentage of the home's sale price paid at closing to the listing agent and to cooperating agents. On closing, the commission is paid 100% to the listing brokerage and then disbursed from there according to the terms of the MLS listing agreement signed by the seller.

Multiple Listing Service (MLS):

The system in which participating brokers agree to share commission on the sale of houses listed by any one of them. Our homes are listed on the Toronto Real Estate Board and then are made available to all 45,000+ licensed Realtors in the Board.

This wide exposure is a major benefit to the seller to give their home maximum exposure to the market.

Condominium:

The ownership of a separate amount of space in a multiple-family dwelling or other multiple-occupancy building with proportioned tenancy in common ownership of common elements used jointly with other owners.

A condo owner owns 100% of the interior of their suite and proportionally shares the ownership of all the common elements (hallways, elevators, lobby, building facilities etc).

Co-operative:

Same as above but the owner does NOT own his/her specific unit. He/she becomes a shareholder of the corporation that owns all the real property and occupies the unit by way of an exclusive tenancy agreement.

Because this type of ownership is a share agreement, it is often more difficult to arrange mortgage financing and typically the buyer is required to put down 20-30% of the purchase price as their down payment.

Mortgage Terms You Should Know

Mortgagee:

The lender (bank or trust company generally).

Mortgagor:

That's you, the borrower.

Blended Payments:

Equal payments monthly or bi-weekly consisting of both a principal and an interest component, paid each month or every two weeks during the term of the mortgage.

Because the principal is being paid down incrementally with each payment, the principal portion of that fixed payment increases each month, while the interest portion decreases, but the total monthly payment does not change.

Closed Mortgage:

A mortgage that cannot be prepaid, renegotiated or refinanced.

Most bank and institutional mortgages we see today are closed with partial pre-payment privileges built into them. If after a few years, you won the lottery and wanted to pay your mortgage off in full, the bank would charge you a penalty.

Open Mortgage:

A mortgage that can be prepaid at any time, without penalty. These are usually private mortgages which have an 'open' privilege.

Mortgage Term:

In a mortgage, "term" is the actual length of time for which the money is loaned, at that rate of interest. At the end of the term, you can either repay the balance of the principal then owing in full or, most commonly, renegotiate the mortgage at the then-current interest rates.

A typical term is 5 years, with anything from 6 months to 5 years also being available.

Amortization:

The number of fixed payments or years it takes to repay the entire amount of the mortgage loan. In Canada, this it typically 25 years.

Principal Balance:

The amount you still owe the lender at any specific time.

Interest Rate:

The return the lender receives for loaning you the money for the mortgage.

Interest rates were as high as 18-21% back in the early 1980's and were in the 4-5% range in the early 2000's. Rates over the past few years have been at record low levels in the mid- to high-2%'s

Amortization Schedule:

The amortization schedule separates out the monthly installment portions for both principal and interest and how much of the payment is allocated to each. It also shows the unpaid principal balance.

The amortization is the number of years that it will take to pay off the mortgage, were the interest rate to remain constant. Mortgage term refers to the length of time a particular interest rate will be in effect.

Conventional mortgage:

A mortgage loan that does not exceed 80% of the appraised value or purchase price of the property, whichever is the lesser. Mortgages that exceed this must be insured and are called high-ratio mortgages.

High-Ratio Mortgage:

This is a mortgage that is higher than 80% of the purchase price (or appraised value) of the property. A high-ratio mortgage typically can be as high as 95% of the value (and in some cases can go to 100% of value). High-ratio mortgages MUST be insured by either CMHC or one of the other two high-ratio mortgage insurers we have available in Ontario.

Mortgage Insurance Premium:
A premium that is added to the mortgage and paid by the borrower over the life of the mortgage. The mortgage insurance insures and protects the mortgage lender against loss in case of default on the part of the borrower.

In our Starbucks Strategy Session or Buyer Consultation we will review what these costs could be for your situation.

Full Mortgage Pre-Approval:
Many people mistakenly believe that by just filling in an online form or having a conversation with a banker where they verbally provide data about their income and their debts is enough to go out and buy a condo or house.

It ABSOLUTELY is not enough and it's very dangerous to buy any home based on just this.

To be 100% sure of your financial capability, and get a FULL mortgage pre-approval, a prospective buyer must provide their banker or mortgage broker with proof of income, proof of down payment and have a credit bureau done. Here's what you'll need to provide...

1- A completed mortgage application form

2- For proof of income, you'll provide a copy of your employment letter, a current pay stub and your last income tax return with T4s and Notice Of Assessment from Revenue Canada

If you are self-employed, you'll need to provide a copy of three years of Revenue Canada tax assessment statements.

3- For proof of down payment, you'll provide a copy of any GICs, term deposits, or RRSPs plus a copy of your bank statement showing current cash in the bank. If you're getting funds from a family member, you'll need to provide a copy of a gift letter signed by that person.

Your lender or mortgage broker will then do a credit check and they will issue an Unconditional Pre-Approval Certificate, which is the lender's guaranteed mortgage commitment to the buyer. It is conditional only upon an appraisal or CMHC/GE Capital approval.

At our Starbucks Strategy Session or Buyer Consultation, we will elaborate on this further and help you make the next steps forward.

Gross Debt Service (GDS) Ratio:
This percentage figure is calculated by totaling the annual payments for mortgage principal, interest, realty taxes and 50% of the heating cost, divided by the gross annual income of the borrower. Most lenders prefer that the GDS be no more than 39%.

Total Debt Service (TDS) Ratio:
This percentage figure is calculated by totaling the annual payments for mortgage principal, interest, realty taxes and 50% of heating costs, PLUS annual payments for bank loans, lines of credit, credit cards & other debts, divided by the borrower's gross annual income. Lenders prefer the TDS be no more than 44%.

P and I:
Principal and interest due on a mortgage.

P I T:
Principal, interest and realty taxes due on a mortgage.

Prepayment Options:
The right to prepay specified amounts of the principal balance (typically 10 - 20% of original mortgage principal amount depending on the lender). Penalty interest rarely may be incurred on those prepayment options. You can often increase your monthly or bi-weekly payments (by from 10-100% depending on the lender) and double-up your payment anytime.

Assumption Agreement:
In this rare case, you might agree to assume an existing mortgage on the property you're buying. The assumption agreement is a legal document signed by the home buyer that requires the buyer to assume responsibility for the obligations of a mortgage made by a former owner.

Mortgage Life Insurance:
Not to be confused with CMHC insurance, life insurance is a form of reducing term insurance recommended for the borrower. In the event of the death of the owner, or one of the owners, the insurance pays off the balance owing on the mortgage. The intent is to protect survivors from losing their homes.

Second Mortgage:
Perhaps, due to credit issues, you can only qualify for a mortgage of up to 75% of the purchase price BUT you only have a 15% down payment. You might then arrange for a second mortgage for the missing 10% of the purchase price.

A second mortgage is usually at a higher interest rate and represents the difference between the price of the house and first mortgage plus the down payment. This may be obtained from private lenders, finance companies or through lawyers and notaries.

Variable Rate Mortgage (Floating Rate):
A mortgage in which payments can be fixed from one to five years, but the interest rate could change from month to month depending on market conditions. Variable mortgage rates are determined by adding or subtracting a certain percentage from the official Bank of Canada Prime Rate.

If interest rates go down, the monthly principal is reduced; if rates go up, the monthly payments might not cover the interest owing and payments may be increased for the next term.

Seller Take Back Mortgage (or Seller Financing):
Although rare in today's low interest, busy market, the seller of a property might provide some or all the mortgage financing to get their property sold.

Default:
Non-payment of the installments due under the terms of the mortgage(s).

Discharge:
The removal of all mortgages and financial encumbrances on a property.

Discharge Penalty:
A sum of money paid to a lender for the privilege of prepaying a mortgage in part or in full.

Mortgage Broker Underwriting Fee:
A sum of money collected by some lenders to offset expenses incurred in the lending transaction.

For 'prime' mortgage borrowers, the lender pays the broker so there is no out-of-pocket cost to the borrower.

However, if the borrower has credit or other issues and the only lenders who will supply the mortgage funds are 'second' or 'third' tier lenders, then there will most likely be a fee attached to the obtaining of that mortgage commitment.

www.ingramcontent.com/pod-product-compliance
Lightning Source LLC
Chambersburg PA
CBHW071444180526
45170CB00001B/446